M000189103

Carried *by* Grace

A guide for mothers of victims of sexual abuse

DEBRA L. BUTTERFIELD

CROSSRIVER
BREWSTER, KANSAS USA

This book is dedicated to my daughter.
You've come so far. I'm proud of you and can hardly
wait to see the blessings God has planned for you.

For every child who has been sexually abused,
there is a mother whose heart is broken.
This book is for you.

Yes, I carried you before you were born.
I will be your God throughout your lifetime —
until your hair is white with age.
I made you, and I will care for you.
I will carry you along and save you. — Isaiah 46:3-4

Be merciful to me, O God, be merciful to me!
For my soul trusts in You;
And in the shadow of Your wings I will make my refuge,
Until these calamities have passed by. — Psalm 57:1

Acknowledgments

Thank you to all who walked this road with me. There will be a jewel in your crown in heaven that proclaims your encouragement, love, and support for me.

A special thank you to Leslie Shaw Holzman, Marilyn Scholz, Ellen Sybert, and Angela Reed Meyer for their editorial work on this book.

To my family, thank you for your love and support.

And to God, who brought me through it all.

Contents

Acknowledgments. 5
You Can Know the End from the Beginning. 9
The Shock of It All. 15
This Can't Be Happening 21
The Question of Why 27
Put Your Faith and Hope in God 33
Conquer Your Fear 39
Anger Management. 45
Seek Prayer Warriors 51
Easing Your Heartache 59
Seek Professional Counsel 63
Recognize False Guilt 69
Stress Relief: the Practical Aspects 75
Stress Relief: the Emotional Aspect 83
Just What Is Forgiveness?. 89
Forgive Yourself. 95
Healing Your Daughter's Heart 99
Acknowledge and Grieve Your Losses 107
Regarding Divorce. 111
Embrace Personal Accountability 115
Regaining Normalcy. 121
Beware Bitterness 127
Learn to Trust Again. 133
The Victim Mentality and Gaining Victory. 141
The Power of Prayer 149
Get Intimate with God 155

Know the Real Enemy. 159
Know Who You Are in Christ 165
The Ebb and Flow of Emotions 169
Appendix A - Prayer of Salvation 175
Appendix B - Five Steps to Finding a Good Lawyer 176
Appendix C - Questions to Ask a Prospective Counselor . . 181
Appendix D - Who I Am in Christ. 183
Appendix E - Additional Resources* 186
Appendix F - How to read through the Psalms in a month . . 189
Appendix G - How to Start a Journal 191
Appendix H - Endnotes 193
About the Author 197

CHAPTER ONE

You Can Know the End from the Beginning

"Can anything separate us from Christ's love? Does it mean
he no longer loves us if we have trouble or calamity, or are
persecuted, or hungry, or destitute, or in danger, or threatened
with death? … No, despite all these things, overwhelming
victory is ours through Christ, who loved us." — Romans 8:35, 37

A shroud of darkness descended on my life one hot August night. My twelve-year-old daughter put a chef's knife to her chest and threatened to kill herself. Her action was an outward sign of the implosion that occurred in her life long before that day. Her step-dad was sexually abusing her. His actions pierced my heart to an unimaginable depth, the scars of which I carry still today, twenty years later.

Sexual abuse is a crime unlike any other. It is a crime that silences not only its victim, but also the victim's family with an almost overwhelming sense of shame. Allow me to illustrate. Imagine someone murdered your child. As horrific as that is, would you feel a need to keep it secret? Would you feel ashamed to tell your friends? Of course you wouldn't. You'd be yelling it from the housetop if you thought it would help the police find the person responsible.

Now think about the present reality. Your husband, or a relative, or friend, has sexually abused your child. Except for the police, who else have you told?

Three heart-wrenching months passed before I told any of my extended family what was happening. If you speak of it openly, you are among the minority. It is this sense of shame — that we are somehow guilty — that keeps us silent. You are not guilty. Your daughter is not guilty. The perpetrator bears the full weight of guilt and responsibility for this crime.

According to the National Center for Victims of Crime, one in five girls and one in twenty boys are abused before the age of eighteen.[1] Other research indicates one in three girls and one in seven boys are abused during their childhood. In as high as ninety-three percent of cases, the victim knew her or his abuser.[2] Sexual abuse is vastly underreported and what constitutes abuse differs, which makes nailing down accurate statistics difficult. Sexual abuse is not limited to physical contact, but can include such things as exposure, voyeurism, and child pornography. The odds are high that either an abuse victim or the mother of a victim is in your circle of friends.

These statistics tell us there are far too many hurting parents out there. When my struggle began, I had been a born-again Christian for fourteen years. I understood a lot about God and knew much of the Bible. Despite that knowledge, I spent too much of my time focused on the problem. My focus kept me mired in fear and drained my emotional, mental, and physical energy. I put on a brave face, but inside, I was an emotional wreck. I believed God would bring my family and me out of the darkness and into the light again; however, my faith vacillated between confidence and doubt.

During the years that followed I discovered promises from God that washed away my doubt. I learned to focus on Him — not the problem — and rest in His peace. "Even when I walk through the darkest valley, I will not be afraid, for you are close beside me." (Psalm 23:4)

We can know the end of our struggle from the beginning. How? Romans 8:37 gives us the answer: victory is ours through Christ. And not just victory, but overwhelming victory. The New King James Version says it this way, "we are more than conquerors." As God's children we can trust the promises He gives us in the Bible. Hallelujah and amen!

You have picked up this book because you find yourself in circumstances similar to mine. The specter of sexual abuse has invaded your life. A family member, a friend, someone you know has sexually abused your child. Grief grips your heart. You may be feeling lost and confused, and you don't know which way to turn for help. Questions about your child's future may plague your mind. Tumultuous emotions buffet you from all sides. All this is normal. It may seem hopeless, but God will provide the wisdom and strength you need.

I can say all that because I have been there. Broken-hearted, tears that seemed endless, a riptide of emotions that threatened to swallow me in the deepest of depression. God carried me through, and He will also bring you and your child through this battle to wholeness again.

As much as I desire to be across the table from you to offer words of comfort and advice, that just isn't possible. That's why I've written this book. By sharing my story here, I hope parents everywhere can find the courage they need to fight this battle and find healing for their child and themselves.

I based this book on the Psalms. Every emotion I've ever experienced I find expressed there. From outrage and revenge to joy and praise, King David's frank confessions served as a guide in my crisis. His words gave voice to my turmoil. When I realized how openly the psalms expressed the same emotions I felt, I returned to them over and over again to lift me up and ease my heartache. I found comfort, guidance, and wisdom.

You and I are sisters in faith, bonded by the experience of sexual abuse against our children. I don't pretend to have all the answers. I am neither a theologian, nor a counselor. I am a mother who looked to God for the answers I needed. I encourage you to do the same. I'm passing on what helped me in hope that it will help you, too.

This book is designed for you, not your child. Yes, your child is wounded, but so are you. And your wounds need healing. I am speaking primarily to the mother whose daughter is the victim, but maybe your son is the victim. A close male or female friend or relative may be the perpetrator. Because in the majority of cases a man is the perpetrator, I refer most often to the perpetrator as him simply in order to avoid the disruptive "him or her" verbiage. Understand, women also sexually abuse. No matter the exact circumstances of your situation, the emotions you experience will be much the same.

The chapters of this book stand alone. You need not read each in succession, but skip around as you desire and need. Each chapter is divided into four sections: My Story, Reflection, Action Steps, and Prayer. The Action Steps are suggestions. You need not complete each, but choose what is best for you, if any. The prayer at the end of each chapter is meant to be a springboard to your prayer time. Use it to get started and continue with your prayer as the Holy Spirit leads you.

I have written this book from the perspective that you have just entered this trial. That your daughter is still a child dependent on your care, rather than an adult now revealing prior abuse. However, the information I present will be of value to you no matter what stage you find yourself in. Additionally, because I sometimes refer to the woman whose husband is the perpetrator, there may be information here that doesn't apply to your situation. By all means, skip those sections.

Just as it is recommended to those grieving the death of a loved one, I recommend you don't make any major changes in your life until you are well into the healing process. The only change that should occur is that if your husband is the perpetrator, he should move out of the house, if he is not already in jail. Circumstances may require contact with your husband. Speaking to him doesn't mean you approve of his wrong behavior.

There should be no contact between your daughter and the abuser, whoever he or she may be, until a counselor deems it is safe. If the perpetrator isn't in therapy and refuses to do therapy, you must distance yourself. This person is not safe for your child, your other children, or you. You must keep your children safe.

Like me, you may feel swallowed by darkness, but take heart, "God is light, and there is no darkness in Him at all." (1 John 1:5) Your journey through this can be one of faith and healing rather than fear and shame. From this day forward draw courage from the fact that nothing separates you from God's love and victory is yours through Christ. With God, you can do this. You and your child will find healing. Victory lies in trusting God to guide you through.

God cannot lie. He says he will never leave us nor forsake us. And when He says everything works together for our good that means *everything* (see Joshua 1:5 and Romans 8:28). Whether you are new to a belief in God or have been walking with Him for many years, seek Him first and foremost in everything.

I pray this book will provide:

- comfort for your pain
- answers to your questions
- practical guidance for daily needs, and
- a pathway to healing your wounds.

In reading this book, I pray you will gain a faith in God deeper than you have ever known.

Have you accepted Jesus as your Savior? If not, there's no better time than now to give your heart to God. Just turn to the prayer of salvation at the back of the book in Appendix A and say the prayer out loud.

Your spirit needs fed on a daily basis just as your physical body does. The Bible, often referred to as the Word, is your spiritual food. It provides you with emotional and mental strength. Spend time reading the Bible daily if possible. For new Christians I recommend starting with the Book of John.

Romans 8:37 mentioned at the beginning of the chapter tells us we have overwhelming victory over our troubles. Together with God, we'll walk the path to healing one day at a time. You will find wholeness again and so will your child. Trust God and stand confident in His promises.

PRAYER

Father, You have created me anew in Christ Jesus. Enable me to hear from You and be obedient to Your voice. Give me spiritual wisdom and insight that I may grow in my knowledge of You. I ask that from Your glorious unlimited resources You empower me with inner strength through the Holy Spirit to stand strong and confident in You as I face my struggles. I put my hope, trust, and confidence in You, Lord. In Jesus' name, amen. *(Eph. 2:16, 3:16, Col. 1:9,10)*

"For everyone who asks receives; he who seeks finds; and to him who knocks, the door will be opened." — Matt. 7:8 (NKJV)

CHAPTER 2

The Shock of It All

"The LORD is close to the brokenhearted." — Psalm 34:18a

MY STORY

W hy did you bring your daughter to the ER?" the nurse asked me.

"She put a knife to her chest and threatened to kill herself."

The nurse escorted us to an examination room. Once there a doctor queried my twelve-year-old daughter, Jenny, with one probing question after another. I remember only one, "Has anyone ever sexually abused you?" and my daughter's unemotional response, "Yes, my step-dad."

The ER doctor sent us to a local psychiatric hospital, admission papers in hand. It was nearly midnight by then, and my daughter faced the same grueling interrogation at the psychiatric hospital. She appeared numb. I tried to listen, yet found myself severed from the painful questioning as if in the midst of an out-of-body experience. The shock of the night's events numbed me mentally and emotionally.

"How could this be happening?" resounded unendingly in my mind long after I said goodbye to Jenny and drove home. My world had collapsed around me. I didn't want to believe my husband had done this, but for my daughter's sake, I knew

I must. I cried the whole thirty minutes it took me to get home.

REFLECTION

When crisis bursts in on us, our first reaction is often shock, just as the body goes into shock after suffering traumatic physical harm such as in a car accident. This is natural and normal — the events we're experiencing are too traumatic for our mind to deal with at that moment. As we reason through our circumstances, our shock fades or we enter denial (more on that later).

I understand the agony life brings. In overcoming life's difficulties I've learned I have two choices that face me each morning when I get out of bed. I can focus on the positive or the negative. That focus determines my mental, emotional, and physical well-being, or lack thereof.

First Peter 5:7 tells us to "give your worries and cares to God, for He cares for you." Jacob, the father of the twelve tribes of Israel, didn't have the Bible to encourage or guide him. How did he handle crisis?

In Genesis 37 we discover Jacob's sons conspiring to kill their brother Joseph. They decide to toss him into a pit to die there. They smear Joseph's tunic, recognizable even from a distance, with goat's blood, and then send it back to Jacob along with a message. Here is my dramatized paraphrase of the account.

"Do you recognize it, Father? Is it your son's tunic?"

Jacob stood stunned, staring at the distinctive colorful coat in his hands. As he pulled open the folds of cloth now crusty with dried blood, his heart sank.

"Yes. There's no mistaking it." Jacob faltered and fell to his knees. "Joseph, Joseph, my beloved son. What wild animal has killed you?" He buried his face in his hands and sobbed. Jacob mourned for many days and though his family tried to comfort him, he refused to be comforted (see Genesis 37 for the full story).

If this were you, what thoughts would be going through your mind? How would you be acting? I'd be shedding crocodile tears and screaming.

In my opinion, Jacob made two mistakes. First, he assumed Joseph had been killed. Why? Wasn't it just as likely that Joseph was injured and lying somewhere waiting for help to arrive? How often do we jump to assumed conclusions when crisis strikes? Secondly, Jacob refused to be comforted. Do we do the same?

King David had a better way. David started out life much like Joseph, as a shepherd boy. He was still a teenager shepherding his father's sheep when Samuel anointed him king of Israel (see 1 Samuel 16:11-12). He was thirty when he ascended the throne (see 2 Samuel 5:4). David saw his share of troubles during the intervening years, but he knew whom to seek when life bore down. "Hear my cry, O God; Attend to my prayer. From the end of the earth I will cry to You, When my heart is overwhelmed; Lead me to the rock that is higher than I." (Psalm 61:1-2 NKJV) David was a man after God's own heart (see Acts 13:22). He knew his help came from God, and he sought God on a continual basis.

No matter what crisis we face we have a choice in how we react. We can be like Jacob and assume the worst and refuse to be comforted, or follow King David's example and turn to God and trust Him to help us in our time of need.

Like my children climbed into my lap for comfort when they were hurt, for three years I approached God as a little child. I mentally climbed into my Father's lap time after time as one crisis after another confronted me and my children as we worked to heal from my husband's crime of abuse. I knew God would listen and not condemn, comfort rather than reprimand, and provide the emotional healing I needed. I asked for strength. I asked for guidance. And I asked Him to mend my broken heart. Over and over again He answered my prayers.

Tragedy has pierced your heart to a depth you never knew existed. You may be in shock about it all. Have you cried so much you feel you have no tears left? I've been there. So have many other mothers. You are not alone. I am with you. God is with you. Shock is a normal reaction. What is important is that you move beyond shock and into the process of managing the crisis.

As Psalm 34:18a states, God is with you. He catches your every tear in a bottle. (Psalm 56:8b) That is love in action! All may seem dark right now, but day by day things will get brighter, and the sun will shine again. You can and will get through this. God understands your pain. He invites you to seek refuge in Him. Climb into the Father's lap and tell Him where it hurts. He loves you and cares for you. He caresses your broken heart with a soothing balm.

ACTION STEPS

Set aside a regular time, daily or weekly, in a quiet spot to tell God everything as Psalm 62:8 advises. It's okay to share your heart and true feelings with Him; He is safe. He loves you unconditionally. Let your tears and words flow freely. Ask for what you need. He will be faithful to answer. Below are some words to get you started.

PRAYER

Abba Father, _____ (name crisis) has entered my life. I am _____ (tell Him exactly how you feel). But You, Lord, are my refuge. I need Your wisdom, guidance, comfort, and _____ (add your specific needs here and continue in your own words). In Jesus' name, amen.

"O my people, trust in Him at all times. Pour out your heart to Him, for God is our refuge." — Psalm 62:8

* For an account of Jacob and Joseph, read Genesis 37

CHAPTER 3

This Can't Be Happening

"But You desire honesty from the womb,
teaching me wisdom even there." — Psalm 51:6

MY STORY

I sat that August morning in the living room staring out the front window. A few days earlier my daughter had threatened suicide and been admitted to a local psychiatric hospital. My husband sat in jail, arrested for sexually abusing her. My eyes burned from a night of tears and fitful sleep. The rosy hues of sunrise promised a warm Colorado summer day, but as I pulled my knees tightly to my chest I felt swallowed by darkness — like Jonah in the belly of the whale. Grief consumed me and fear of what was ahead nearly paralyzed me. In my grief, I cried out to God. This can't be happening.

The day I drove to my husband's arraignment the situation began to sink in. Seeing him in that felony orange jumpsuit mortified me. A waking nightmare had descended on our lives.

REFLECTION

Like any parent, God wants the best for us, but our finite minds struggle to understand how a crisis could possibly be good. I wanted God to wave a magic wand and make it all go away.

Webster's New Universal Unabridged Dictionary defines

denial as "an assertion that something said, believed, alleged, etc., is false.[1]" At minddisorders.com denial is defined as "the refusal to acknowledge the existence or severity of unpleasant external realities or internal thoughts and feelings.[2]" Denial is a defense mechanism that protects our psychological well-being from the initial shock of traumatic events. But it is essential for one's mental, physical, and emotional well-being to move past denial and on to acceptance.

Denial is refusal to acknowledge there is a battle raging. Consequently the person in denial is not fighting the battle spiritually, mentally, or emotionally either. Acceptance of a situation isn't giving up. It's choosing to enter the ring and fight. In acceptance, our first step is to trust God. "And we know that God causes everything to work together for the good of those who love God and are called according to his purpose for them." (Romans 8:28)

Next, tap into God's grace. "And He said to me, 'My grace is sufficient for you, for My strength is made perfect in weakness.' Therefore most gladly I will rather boast in my infirmities, that the power of Christ may rest upon me." (2 Corinthians 12:9 NKJV). Most often when grace is spoken of or taught, it is to say grace is God's unmerited favor given freely, but this verse shows us that grace is also God's power. This grace that is sufficient is His strength and power. I especially like the way author and speaker Joyce Meyer explains grace in her book *If Not for the Grace of God*: "Grace is the power of God available to meet our needs without any cost to us. It is received by believing, rather than through human effort.[3]" To receive God's power, simply ask for Him to provide it. "You can ask for anything in my name, and I will do it, so that the Son can bring glory to the Father." (John 14:13)

Not wanting to believe and refusing to believe are two very

different things. I didn't want to believe my husband could do such a vile thing. Nonetheless, I did accept it. Refusal to believe a problem actually exists despite evidence to the contrary is denial, and carried to extremes can cause psychological issues. Denial doesn't make the situation go away. Once a traumatic situation is accepted, we can resolve to take appropriate action to make things better.

You are probably asking yourself could it be true that a family member or friend really sexually abused your child? You may be wondering how long has it been happening, and why it happened at all. A police investigation may determine the answer to the first two questions, but not the third. At the most basic level, the reason the abuser committed this crime is because his needs, whether physical or psychological, controlled him just as drugs and alcohol control an addict.

"Why did God allow it to happen?" is something about God's actions we may find out when we enter heaven (more on this later). Continually asking why mires us in the problem and in our grief, and is potent fertilizer for bitterness. You can rant and cry and scream at God. I know I did, but here's what I learned: God allows difficulties in our lives to help us grow. Romans 8:28 tells us God takes everything in our lives, the good and the bad, and uses it for our good. He will use this situation to grow your daughter into the woman He has destined her to be.

Use your emotional energy to seek the truth, however gruesome, rather than denying the situation. Your determination for truth gives you focus and enables you to make wise decisions. God has a plan, a future, and hope for each of us (see Jeremiah 29:11). He has one for your child, too. Remember, your child was first God's child. He loves each of our children with a love far above anything we can imagine.

Most likely this abuse came to light because your daughter had

23

the courage to say she was being abused. If you deny the situation, you can send the wrong message to your injured child: "You don't believe me or support me." She may recant (say it really didn't happen after all) or completely shut down. This puts her at risk for continued abuse. Whether you believe in the perpetrator's innocence or guilt isn't the issue. What is at issue is that you acknowledge the situation exists. Accepting the truth of your daughter's words sends two very important messages to her: (1) I believe you; (2) I'm getting help to make the abuse stop.

We can't see the future, but God does. For Him time is non-existent. He sees the end from the beginning and everything in between. He sees every individual thread that creates the tapestry, every dab of color that paints the final portrait, every atom of the trillions of cells that build your body. Whatever comparison you want to make, God knows the minute details of our lives.

He calms our storm…not the storm around us, but the storm within us. When you focus on Him you open the door for His peace to enter. Counter the problem by encouraging yourself with God's promises. Trusting Him and His promises gives you strength. Isaiah 26:3 tells us "You [the LORD] will keep in perfect peace all who trust in you, all whose thoughts are fixed on you!"

As you face your situation, here are some practical suggestions to help.

• Enlist prayer partners who will support you regularly in prayer.

• Ask for help from your support network (family, friends who are willing to help). Babysitting, cleaning, laundry, cooking meals, whatever you need. See the chapter "Seek Prayer Warriors," for more information on support networks.

• Take care of yourself physically, emotionally, and mentally. Stress compromises your immune system making you more susceptible to illness. Refer to the chapters on stress relief for more specific help in this area.

• Get at least eight hours of sleep every night; rest allows your body to re-energize.

• Laugh. There are physically healing benefits in laughter.

It's okay to cry. I cried so much there were times I thought I had cried myself dry, and still there were tears. Our God is an awesome God. He will give you the strength and guidance you need. Just ask. All things are possible for Him.

ACTION STEPS

• Allow the proper authorities to investigate the abuse allegations and cooperate with their investigation.

• Support your daughter. It is vital for her to know you believe her.

• Seek professional help if needed. Determine to accept the situation and work toward healing.

• Ask for help from those you trust.

PRAYER

Father, the Bible says all things hidden will be revealed and come to light. Shine Your light where darkness reigns. Reveal the truth of this situation and make the details known to those concerned. Be with me, heavenly Father. Give me the strength I need to accept this situation. Be with my family as we face this together. In Jesus' name, amen. *(Mark 4:22)*

"Oh, send out Your light and Your truth!
Let them lead me." — Psalm 43:3 (NKJV)

CHAPTER 4

The Question of Why

"Yes, You have been with me from birth; from my mother's womb You have cared for me." — Psalm 71:6

MY STORY

W hy did God let this happen? He could have prevented it," I said to my closest friend. I was praying for God's help, but all that seemed to come was more trouble. I felt empty, my trust in God betrayed.

"Deb, remember. For eight months before this all began, we prayed for God to bring your backslidden husband back to Him," my friend said. This woman was my prayer partner. She bolstered me when I had no strength left to pray, pointed out wisdom from the Bible, and encouraged me. This particular morning she quoted Romans 8:28 to me. I couldn't see God's hand at work, nor could I imagine how He would take this mess and bring good from it. But, like Job, I determined I would trust God no matter what.

From that day on as I waited for answers, I embraced the difficulties. It wasn't important to understand why it happened, but simply to focus on the spiritual and emotional growth to be gained during the struggle. I stopped asking God to make things better and started asking, "What do You want me to learn through this?"

REFLECTION

When tragedy strikes, we often ask why. God is okay with us asking the question, but He doesn't want us to get stuck there. Getting stuck opens the door to bitterness. Like a pernicious weed, bitterness invades our lives, wraps its tentacles around our spirit, and chokes our faith. Beware!

Let's look at the question of why from a different angle.

God saw my husband abusing my daughter, but I didn't. If God had not infused my daughter with the courage to speak out, my husband would have continued with his abuse, further injuring my daughter. The revelation of my husband's actions saved my daughter from five more years of abuse.

Why did God allow my husband to abuse in the first place?

John 3:16 tells us God sent Jesus to die for us. He paid the highest price anyone could pay to redeem us so we can once again have fellowship with Him. After paying a price like that would He be lackadaisical in His attitude toward us? Would He just step back and watch as life happened? No! God loves us with an everlasting love (see Jeremiah 31:3). He promises never to leave us or forsake us (see Joshua 1:5).

We live in a fallen world filled with sin. God has given each of us free will — the power to make our own decisions — because He wants us to choose to love and obey Him. He doesn't want puppets who love Him because they have no choice. Free will means *we* choose what we do, who we love, and whether or not to believe in and obey God. My husband made the choice to abuse. He was acting within his free will. No one forced him, though the devil probably did plenty of tempting. Unfortunately my husband chose my daughter. God is grieved that my daughter (and yours) was hurt. He is also grieved at

28

my ex-husband's choice. But I can say with utmost confidence that God is in the midst of it all. He wants the perpetrator to repent and turn from this sin. He wants your daughter to heal.

OK, you say, so God loves us and has given us free will, but that still doesn't answer the question of why God allowed this to happen.

Living in Colorado Springs, Colorado, for fourteen years I had a daily view of Pike's Peak from the front porch of my house. When I drove to the top of the Peak, I gained an amazing view of the city and surrounding area. We all love a mountaintop experience. Who can deny the beauty of the world when seen from above? It's that awe-inspiring view many people think about when they imagine being on the mountaintop.

While we're on the mountain, we are physically separated from the chaos and worries of the world. Laid out before us is the grandeur of nature, not the frustration of bumper-to-bumper traffic, or the danger of crime, or the uncertainty of the economy. We may see the city smog, but we are above it where the sun shines brightly and bathes us in its warmth.

When we speak metaphorically of having a mountaintop experience, we are mentally and emotionally above the day-to-day problems in life. Everything is going right, and usually something amazing has happened in our life — we just got married, or had a baby, or succeeded in reaching a major goal. We are closer to God and sense His presence more keenly because our problems aren't there to distract us. We can bask in His light and His love. He cleanses us by washing away the grime that weighs us down. We rest when we're on the mountain. We need that cleansing and rest!

Many people, including me, want to stay on the mountain because we don't want to have problems in our lives. But just like we get up each morning after resting for the night, we must get up and come down from the mountain. Would the Israelites have received the Ten Commandments or been led to the Promised Land if Moses had stayed on the mountain?

Living in the high altitude of Colorado taught me the mountaintop has its drawbacks.

The air is thinner.

In other words, there are fewer molecules of oxygen per square inch. Your body must adjust. Depending on how physically fit you are, you might experience altitude sickness within the first few days of being at a higher altitude. Colorado Springs' altitude is 6032 feet. I was five months pregnant when we moved there, and I experienced the flu-like symptoms of altitude sickness my first week there. My Lamaze childbirth instructor told me I probably wouldn't acclimate until after I had

> # God never wastes pain. He always uses it to accomplish His purpose. And His purpose is for His glory and our good.
>
> *~Jerry Bridges*

my baby. I had so much difficulty with the breathing exercises, she recommended I stop the class. That's how much the high altitude can affect you.

Very little grows on the mountaintop.

The right conditions must exist for growth — fertile soil, water, air. Above a certain altitude the trees stop growing. It's called the tree line. From a distance this point appears distinct, but of course it is a gradual change. Without getting into the science of nature, suffice to say, very little grows above the tree line. What does grow is only noticeable to those on the mountain, not to those who view it from a distance.

God does not willingly bring affliction or grief to us. He does not delight in causing us to experience pain or heartache. He always has a purpose for the grief He brings or allows to come into our lives. Most often we do not know what that purpose is, but it is enough to know that His infinite wisdom and perfect love have determined that the particular sorrow is best for us. God never wastes pain. He always uses it to accomplish His purpose. And His purpose is for His glory and our good.[1] *~Jerry Bridges*

We grow and mature emotionally and spiritually through the difficulties we face in life. We find those conditions in our day-to-day lives, not on the mountaintop. God has a purpose for us. He allows difficulties because He knows the ideal conditions needed for each of us as individuals to accomplish His destiny for us.

As you take this journey, let go of "why?" Take God's hand and walk with Him. He is sovereign; He knows everything that's happening. Allow Him to do what He did for me: To pick you up in His arms and carry you through with His grace. He will provide you with His strength for each day and His wisdom for the choices you must make. He will lead you to the point where you can, with a sincere heart, say "What do You want me to learn through this situation?" And you will be able to release your daughter into His hands to work His miraculous healing in His way.

ACTION STEPS

- Stay focused on God, not on the situation. Keep the end in mind: healing and wholeness for your daughter, you, and your family.
- Pray and believe you have received the answers. Thank God everyday for His answers.
- Do your best to view difficult times as opportunities to grow — personally, relationally, spiritually.
- If you don't already keep a journal, consider starting one. See Appendix G for more information.

PRAYER

Heavenly Father, You are holy and righteous. There is so much about this situation I don't understand, but You see it all from the perspective of eternity. I don't know what good things You have planned for my daughter, but You do. She is Your masterpiece. Thank You, Lord, that through Your mighty power at work in us, You accomplish infinitely more than I might ask or imagine. Provide Your strength when I am weak. Help me to let go of "why?". Comfort my aching heart. In Jesus' name, amen. *(Eph. 2:10, 3:20)*

"Praise the Lord; praise God our savior!
For each day he carries us in his arms." — Psalm 68:19

CHAPTER 5

Put Your Faith and Hope in God

"Forever, O LORD, Your word is settled in heaven. Your faithfulness endures to all generations." — Psalm 119:89-90a

MY STORY

Y ou're charged with three counts of sexual molestation. How do you plead?" asked the judge.

"Guilty," my husband answered.

For months I'd been praying for God to do whatever it took to bring my husband back in relationship with Jesus. I never imagined this nightmare. Without my hope and faith in God, I would have given up the fight.

REFLECTION

In today's society the word hope is almost synonymous with wish. Hope carries a "maybe so" connotation. In the Bible hope means confident expectation. To hope — to have confident expectation — we need to know what to expect. Throughout the Bible God gives His followers a vision of His plans. Abraham couldn't grasp how he could become the father of many nations when he had no child. God told him to count the stars

— an impossible task — in order to give Abraham a vision of His promise. (See Genesis 15:5) He told the Hebrews in Egypt He was taking them to a land flowing with milk and honey. (See Exodus 3:8) In each case, what followed was hope, the confident expectation that God would do what He said, even though they could not see this promise with their natural eye.

John 3:16 tells us we have eternal life when we believe in Jesus. Philippians 3:20 tells us our home is in heaven. And Revelation 21 is filled with descriptions of heaven. These verses give us a picture of what God has ahead for us. They give us the foundation we need for our hope, our confident expectation in God.

Trusting God to fulfill His promise is an act of faith. (See 2 Corinthians 5:7) But what is faith exactly? *Webster's New Universal Unabridged Dictionary* tells us faith is (1) confidence or trust in a person or thing; (2) belief that is not based on proof.[1] Hebrews 11:1 tells us that faith is the confidence that what we expect to happen will happen. Faith is the act of believing something we cannot see with our natural eyes. God has given each of us a measure of faith (see Romans 12:3) and it was that measure of faith you drew upon when you accepted Christ as your savior. We have not seen God, yet believe in God. The disciples walked with Jesus Christ, God incarnate. We have their written word — the Bible — inspired by God to guide and teach us.

Faith is not the power of God, but is the channel He uses to deliver His power. Let me explain. You've gone to the store and purchased a large screen HDTV. You bring it home, pull it out of the box, set it on the table, and turn it on. Nothing happens. Wait a minute, in your excitement you forgot to plug it in. You take the cord and plug it into the outlet. The electrical power from that outlet runs through the cord to the inner workings of the TV. God is our source of power, and our faith is like that electrical cord connecting us to God's power and allowing that power to flow from Him to us.

To our finite mind, God works in mysterious ways, and though His holiness is too glorious for us to behold, God does not shroud Himself in mystery. He reveals who He is in the Bible. Below are several names of God that communicate attributes of His being and His work in our lives.

- Yahweh Shammah, the LORD Is There. He is always with us. See Ezekiel 48:35.
- Yahweh-Yireh, the LORD will provide. God provides for our needs. See Genesis 22:14.
- Yahweh-Shalom, the LORD is peace. God gives us peace. We need not worry or fear. See Judges 6:24.
- Yahweh Tsidqenu, The LORD Is Our Righteousness. As the righteous judge, God accepts Christ's sacrifice as payment for our sins. When we accept Jesus as our Savior we become righteous. See Jeremiah 23:6, 33:16, and Romans 5:17.
- "I am the LORD who heals you." (Exodus 15:26) He heals us spiritually, physically, mentally, and emotionally. See also Psalm 103:2-3 and Psalm 147:3.
- He is our shepherd, the one who takes care of us. See Psalm 23, Ezekiel 34:12, and John 10:11.

All we need, God is, and God is all we need.

God also reveals His plans in the Bible: To give the Hebrews a land of their own, to give us spiritual gifts (see 1 Corinthians 12:7), to gather all believers to Him (see 1 Thessalonians 4:16-17), that He will return to earth (see Acts 1:9-11). He reveals so much more. From Genesis to Revelation God tells us His plans.

Let's take a look at God's faithfulness.

To be faithful is to be "true to one's word, promises, vows, etc." and "reliable, trusted or believed."[2] God is not a liar. (See Numbers 23:19 and Hebrews 6:18-19) If He lied everything else about His being would unravel. Because God is true to His word you can trust Him to do what He says He will do.

Are you struggling to believe in His faithfulness? Here is a passage you can memorize and on which you can meditate: "The faithful love of the LORD never ends! His mercies never cease. Great is his faithfulness; his mercies begin afresh each morning." (Lamentations 3:22-23)

If God made Himself a mystery, how could we come to know Him? If He didn't reveal His plans and promises, how could we have hope and faith in Him? God has opened wide the door to knowing Him and what He has for us. We only have to enter.

In literature and in Scripture, life is depicted as a race. How we choose to run the race determines our quality of life, and whom or what we choose to run toward determines our peace and joy. [3] *~ Cynthia Heald*

Like many things in life, belief in the God of the Bible is a choice. I can't remember a time when I did not believe God existed. For others, belief is more difficult. One can study the religious texts of the world and sit at the feet of religious scholars and be taught, but one's belief still comes down to choice. God helps us every way He can. He gave us the Bible to help us come to know Him, and He speaks to us through prayer. My life experiences have proved to me He does what the Bible says He'll do.

There are many of God's promises we have yet to see. There are also many we have seen. For those we have not seen, we have hope, confident expectation they will occur at some point in the future. Life may seem dark right now, but have hope and faith in God. He will light your way. "Your word is a lamp to my feet and a light to my path." (Psalm 119:105) Just as your muscles grow strong through exercise, your confidence and trust in God will grow as you face life's obstacles with God one day at a time.

Even with my faith in God, there were times when I wanted to give up. Difficulties seemed to pile up, and prayers seemed unanswered. Sometimes I had a short sulk — sometimes a long one — and cried. Sometimes I would call my prayer warriors and ask for extra prayer. I would read promise verses to encourage myself. Most often, and especially when I felt the threat of a nervous breakdown, I cried out to God with the simple words "help me, I need Your strength for today." He always provided.

In literature and in Scripture, life is depicted as a race. How we choose to run the race determines our quality of life, and whom or what we choose to run toward determines our peace and joy.

~Cynthia Heald

ACTION STEPS

- Before you even get out of bed each day ask God to be with you and provide the strength you need for whatever the day holds in store for you.
- The Bible is brimming with promises from God. Find verses that speak to you. Most often, a verse will jump out at you as you read, but I've listed several below to help you. Write them out on a piece of paper or put them into your smart phone. Whatever method you choose, keep these verses ac-

cessible so you can read them whenever you feel the need.

- There are many Bible promise books that list the various promises in the Bible. Consider purchasing one so you have God's promises available wherever you are and whenever you need them.

PROMISE VERSES

"The LORD says, 'I will rescue those who love Me. I will protect those who trust in My name.'" Psalm 91:14

"Don't be afraid, for I am with you. Don't be discouraged, for I am your God. I will strengthen you and help you. I will hold you with My victorious right hand." Isaiah 41:10

"Ask, and it will be given to you; seek, and you will find; knock, and it will be opened to you. For everyone who asks receives, and he who seeks finds, and to him who knocks it will be opened." Matthew 7:7-8 NKJV

"I have come as a light to shine in this dark world, so that all who put their trust in me will no longer remain in the dark." John 12:46

PRAYER

Heavenly Father, I don't understand what You're doing in this situation, but I trust You. Help my unbelief. Lead me to verses that will help me stand firm in this battle. Help me know You want only what is best for my family and me, and that You will take what Satan has intended for evil and bring good from it. Guide me, give me wisdom, help me trust You. In Jesus' name, amen.

"How great is the goodness You have stored up for those who fear You. You lavish it on those who come to You for protection, blessing them before the watching world." — Psalm 31:19

CHAPTER 6

Conquer Your Fear

*"I will look up to the mountains — does my help come from
there? My help comes from the LORD." (Psalm 121:1-2)*

MY STORY

How could this be happening? I must have asked myself
that question a dozen times a day. It didn't seem possible. When my husband confessed his guilt, new questions moved in: What happens now? What if the police charge
me as an accomplice? What if Social Services takes my children
away from me? What if I can't pay the mortgage? One what-if
scenario after another stampeded through my thoughts.

Fear tried to control me.

REFLECTION

What-ifs are fears about something that hasn't happened
and probably won't. If I was to name what I believe is the most
destructive force in the world, it would be fear. This emotion
wields great power, stopping many people from taking action,
and driving others to unthinkable acts of horror.

Fear is a reaction to a perceived danger, real or unreal, and
triggers certain chemical reactions in the body often referred
to as the fight-or-flight response. The hormones released into
the body prepare us to stay and fight or run away from the

danger. This innate response was designed to help protect mankind from the physical danger of wild animals. Today's dangers are mostly psychological — job loss, economic woes, terrorism — but the body still reacts the same:

- Respiratory rate increases
- Pupils dilate
- Eyesight sharpens
- Perception of pain diminishes
- Blood is directed into our muscles and limbs and away from our digestive tract.

According to Dr. Neil Neimark of the Body Soul Connection, "When our fight or flight system is activated, we tend to perceive everything in our environment as a possible threat to our survival. By its very nature, the fight or flight system bypasses our rational mind — where our more well thought out beliefs exist — and moves us into 'attack' mode… Our fear is exaggerated. Our thinking is distorted. We see everything through the filter of possible danger."[1]

I faced many unknowns in those first few days after my husband was arrested. He was in the military and the civil authorities relinquished their jurisdiction over to the military. What authority or jurisdiction did the military prosecutor have in charging me with abuse? He was convinced I knew about and allowed my husband to abuse my daughter. What would happen to my two-year-old if I was arrested? Would county authorities take him away and place him in foster care? How was I going to pay all the hospital and lawyer bills if my husband was sent to prison?

It was as if a nuclear bomb had been dropped. I knew our lives would never be the same again. The police, the military investigators, the social workers, and the civil lawyers all became the enemy trying to take away my three children and send me off to prison along with my husband. I experienced the physical symptoms of fight or flight often. Only my closest church friends and family escaped my constant "is this the enemy" scrutiny. Too often I focused on my fears, those what-ifs, rather than rationally thinking through the situation.

Let's examine fear from a spiritual perspective. Second Timothy 1:7 tells us God did not give us a "spirit of fear and timidity." The objective of intimidation is to deter you from action and coerce you into submitting to the authority of the intimidator. The intimidator accomplishes this task by crushing you with a sense of inferiority and fear. These are actions an abuser uses against a victim. Satan wants us intimidated. He wants to defeat us and keep us cowering in the corner. Since God is not the one who makes us afraid, we can logically deduce that fear and timidity come from Satan.

The other half of 2 Timothy 1:7 says God gave us a spirit "of power and of love and of a sound mind." He has also given us authority over Satan: "I have given you authority over all the power of the enemy." (Luke 10:19) If we allow fear to control us, we are relinquishing our God-given authority and allowing Satan to control us.

In the story of Peter and his walk on the water, God gives us an example of how to handle our fear. (See Matthew 14:22-33) The disciples were crossing the Galilee Sea. Jesus stayed behind to pray. In the darkness of night, He came to them walking on the water. The disciples' first reaction was fear — a natural reaction to something unknown. Jesus called out to them telling them it was He and not to be afraid. Peter wanted to know it was really Jesus. "Lord, if it's really You, tell me to come to You, walking on the water." Jesus said yes. A wind raged all around them. Waves rocked the boat, but Peter stepped out in faith, his eyes on Jesus, and walked on water. But when Peter took his eyes off Jesus and looked at the formidable conditions around him, he began to sink.

You may be thinking "Peter, why did you take your eyes off Jesus?" But how often do we take our eyes off Christ and look at the storm raging around us?

What did Peter do when he began to sink? He called out to Jesus to save him. Jesus reached out and grabbed Peter and they climbed into the boat — and the wind stopped.

Where are your thoughts focused? Fear fills us when we focus on the wind and the waves and like Peter, we sink. Be conscious of what you are thinking! That's where the battle begins. It is our faith in God that keeps us afloat.

We conquer fear by remembering God has given us power and authority over fear. We use our sound mind to think rationally and recognize fear is a only a feeling, not a tangible object that can wound us. We give fear power in our lives by yielding to it. Place your confidence and your focus on God. He calms our storm.

ACTION STEPS

- Start your day with a devotional reading.
- Take one day at a time. Matthew 6:34 tells us not to worry about tomorrow.
- Spend time each day to bring your thoughts into focus. When we focus on Christ and His promises we find peace in the midst of the storm.
- If you find yourself dwelling on what-ifs, stop and take control of your thoughts and the spirit of fear. (See 2 Corinthians 10:5 and James 4:7)
- Analyze your fears rationally and remind yourself of

God's promises to care for you.

• Encourage yourself with Bible verses specific to your situation. Keep them handy and read them whenever the need arises. I posted some on my refrigerator, others I kept with my Bible. I read them every day. Create as many as you like. Insert yourself into the verse. I've given you several verses below with which to start.

"God is our [my] refuge and strength, a very present help in trouble. Therefore we [I] will not fear." — Psalm 46:1 (NKJV)

"The LORD is my light and my salvation; Whom shall I fear? The LORD is the strength of my life; Of whom shall I be afraid?" — Psalm 27:1 (NKJV) *This verse is a particular favorite of mine.*

"Whenever I am afraid, I will trust in You." — Psalm 56:3 (NKJV)

"Fear not, for I am with you; be not dismayed, for I am your God. I will strengthen you, yes, I will help you, I will uphold you with my righteous right hand." —Isaiah 41:10 (NKJV). *This is God's promise to you.*

PRAYER

Dear Lord, thank You for giving me power, love, and a sound mind. Because I trust in You I can be bold and courageous. I take command over the spirit of fear. It no longer controls me or my family. Give me wisdom and help me make godly decisions. You are my helper. In Jesus' name, amen.

"I prayed to the LORD, and He answered me.
He freed me from all my fears." — Psalm 34:4

CHAPTER 7

Anger Management

*"Be angry, and do not sin. Meditate within your heart
on your bed, and be still." — Psalm 4:4 (NKJV)*

MY STORY

God, I'm so angry at You for letting this happen," I
screamed one morning during my prayer time. I
knew I couldn't hide my anger from God — He's omniscient (all-knowing). All the same I kept my anger seething
within me for months. Then one day while my two-year-old
napped, I closeted myself in my bedroom and screamed those
very words at God. I held nothing back. I told Him exactly
how I felt. Then I cried.

REFLECTION

Have you thought these same words? Even if you want to
say them and don't, God knows how you feel. God is patient
and loving. He listens to our ranting without condemning us.
Once I released this poisonous anger, my body felt better. It
wasn't the proverbial 200 pound weight off my shoulders, but
a boulder out of the pit of my stomach. My tears spent, I continued in prayer. Before I finished I was praising and thanking
God for the refining work He was doing in my life.

Confessing my anger was easy, but I didn't expect what

happened next — the anger at God disappeared. Like piercing a throbbing water blister, the pain of my emotions drained away. The emotion no longer overwhelmed my thoughts, and my mind was open to hear what God had to tell me. I stopped asking why did this happen and started asking Him to show me what lessons he had for me to learn. I began to trust Him to work His will in my life.

From that day forward my conversations with God became sounding boards. I expressed my varied emotions to Him. I discovered that oftentimes all I needed was to express myself. Once said, my mind could view the situation objectively and find answers. I could resolve the issue and move forward. My faith and confidence in God grew.

In expressing ourselves to God, we should always remember who He is — our Creator. "Don't be afraid of those who want to kill your body; they cannot touch your soul. Fear only God, who can destroy both soul and body in hell." (Matt. 10:28) To fear God doesn't mean to be scared, but to be in awe, to revere.

God is omnipotent (all-powerful). It was within His power to stop the incest from ever happening. But then He would be violating His rule of free will. God doesn't want puppets. He wants us to come to Him, love Him, and obey Him, not because He forces us to but because we choose to do so.

The New Living Translation states Psalm 4:4 thus: "Don't sin by letting anger control you." It's okay to be angry. It is when we let anger control us that we enter the realm of sin. Lashing out verbally or physically, seeking revenge, and holding a grudge are unhealthy ways to handle anger. In fact, these methods of anger management are veiled attempts at manipulating the person with whom you are angry.

The other half of Psalm 4:4 (NLT) gives us an answer on

how to handle our anger: "Think about it overnight and re-main silent." No, this isn't saying stew about what you're angry over. It means rationally think through the situation and discern why you are angry. Then you can determine how to resolve the situation assertively. This process allows you to *act* calmly at a later time, rather than *react* emotionally during the heat of anger when you may say something you'll later regret.

Assertiveness is the healthiest way to manage anger. Assertiveness requires that you know your needs and how to clearly express those needs without hurting others. That's where "meditating within your heart" comes in. King David was a man after God's own heart, and he meditated often.

To meditate is to think about, reflect on, consider. Meditate also carries a spiritual definition. Whereas for many Eastern religions, meditation means emptying the mind of all thought, for the Christian, it refers to rational thought about a particular Bible verse and what it has to say to us. (See Psalm 119:15-16) If the word "meditate" bothers you, replace it with the word "ponder," defined by Webster's as "to consider something deeply and thoroughly."[1]

To ponder your situation is not thinking about who is wrong and who is right, or mulling over each wrong action and growing angrier.

Pondering is sane, objective thought about actions and words said and asking yourself why you feel about them the way you do.

- With whom am I angry?
- Why am I angry?
- What are my needs in this particular situation?
- Why do I feel those needs are at risk?
- How can I accurately and calmly communicate those

47

needs in an appropriate manner that is not demeaning?

I didn't learn assertiveness as I child. In fact, I'm still learning how to be assertive. If you struggle with being assertive, there are numerous books on assertiveness as well as classes that can help. Like all new skills, it takes practice to get better.

Another anger management method is called suppression — to hold it in and convert it to a more constructive behavior, such as going for a fast walk, or washing the dishes. However, there are risks to this technique. Just as in the fight or flight response I discussed earlier in the book, anger has physical effects on the body. If anger isn't allowed an outward physical expression it can turn inward and lead to problems such as high blood pressure and depression. Don't confuse suppressing anger with stuffing it. I usually stuffed my anger — didn't express it, think about it, or convert it. It led to depression.

Staying angry at the perpetrator doesn't hurt him — unless you are behaving aggressively toward him or her through your actions or words. Staying angry hurts you because it opens the door to bitterness and places stress on your body that can break down your immune system.

Even after learning healthy techniques to resolve anger, I still struggle with stuffing it. Like changing bad habits for good, learning new techniques for coping with your anger takes time and effort. Resolving your anger in a healthy manner benefits both you and your family.

ACTION STEPS

• Are you angry at God for past or present circumstances? Confess it to Him in your prayer time today. Don't be afraid to express it the way you feel it. If you need to shout, then shout. Do this in a private place where you won't be interrupted or overheard. Don't stay angry. If at all possible, do not leave your prayer time until you have resolved your anger toward God and can end your prayer with praise for God's infinite wisdom and work in your life. "Do not let the sun go down on your wrath." (Eph. 4:26 NKJV)

• Utilize anger management. If you tend to handle your anger in unhealthy ways, seek help. A counselor can give you insight into your anger weaknesses and techniques for changes as well as guidance on quality programs or books. The local librarian can help you locate any books the library may carry. Do some research on the Internet or consider purchasing a book or enrolling in an anger management class. If you already handle your anger assertively, you are ahead of the game!

• As you meditate/ponder, ask yourself the bulleted questions in the above text. Discover what is at the root of your anger. Journal your questions and answers, then fashion an assertive response. Mentally rehearse your response before actually speaking to the person involved.

• Talk to God and ask His guidance. He should always be the first one we seek help from.

• You'll find that staying calm and assertive in all your relationships removes stress and tension from your body. It also places responsibility for action in the lap of those who are truly responsible.

• For more information on anger visit the American Psychological Association Web site, www.apa.org/topics/anger/control.aspx

• If you struggle with "why?" refer back to the chapter "The Question of Why" and reread it.

PRAYER

God, I'm so angry at You for allowing my child to be hurt, but I know You didn't cause it and aren't happy about it either. Be with me, guide me, and help me manage my anger in positive, healthy ways. Bring spiritual, emotional, and physical healing to my family and me. I praise and thank You for who You are. You are holy, all-powerful and all-knowing and deserve my praise and worship. Holy Spirit, help me understand why I'm angry and show me positive ways my needs can be met. Help me assertively express myself. In Jesus' name, amen.

"Stop being angry! Turn from your rage! Do not lose your temper — it only leads to harm." — Psalm 37:8

CHAPTER 8

Seek Prayer Warriors

"The LORD says, 'I will guide you along the best pathway for your life. I will advise you and watch over you.'" — *Psalm 32:8*

MY STORY

A fire gutted our basement. My two-year-old son got sick with severe diarrhea. The police, social workers, and military investigators weekly paraded to the house to question me. The only decisions I felt capable of were when to change my son's cloth diaper and whether to do the laundry.

Life was an out-of-control roller coaster, and I had the front seat.

REFLECTION

"Why do you go running off to your friend every time we have an argument?" my first husband once asked me. We'd been married less than a year. Maybe he thought I was crying to my friend about what a miserable husband I had, but I wasn't. I was seeking advice on how to handle the situation. This friend was a part of my support system.

The weight of a crisis is an emotional, mental, and physical burden too heavy to bear alone. Having a support system to share the burden helps us bear the myriad of circumstances involved in any crisis.

A support system is a network of people who care about you and your success in life. They are joyful, not jealous, when you reach your goals; will listen when you need to talk; provide help and encouragement; and, like a sports coach, give tough advice that helps you grow. They're available to give you a ride when your car breaks down, or to fix a meal for your family when a loved one is in the hospital. Psychotherapist Will Baum, blogger for *Psychology Today*, says, "Getting help from others is often the first, best step toward getting through a crisis."[1]

Let's look at two stories from the Bible.

In Exodus 17:9-13 we find Joshua and the Israelites engaged in battle with the Amalekites. Moses, Aaron, and Hur have gone to the top of a hill where they have full view of the battle. Here, on the top of this hill, Moses prayed for their victory. When Moses held up his hand, Israel prevailed in the battle. When Moses let down his hand, Amalek prevailed. "But Moses' hands became heavy; so they took a stone and put it under him, and he sat on it. And Aaron and Hur supported his hands, one on one side, and the other on the other side; and his hands were steady until the going down of the sun. So Joshua defeated Amalek and his people with the edge of the sword." (Exodus 17:12-13)

Now let's turn to the New Testament in Matthew. Jesus has asked Peter, James, and John to pray with him in the Gar-

> "Getting help from others is often the first, best step toward getting through a crisis."
>
> ~*Will Baum*

den of Gethsemane. (See Matthew 26:38) Jesus wanted their prayers for the ordeal ahead — His crucifixion. Peter, James, and John did pray, but sleep overtook them. On a side note, understand we all have our limitations.

If the children of Israel and Jesus as fully man sought prayer from others, how much more do we need that kind of help? There are some battles in our lives that require the help of others, and this is one of them. Prayer is our No. 1 weapon, connecting us to God, His power, and His peace.

God does not expect us to fight alone. As created in the image of God, we are relational beings and relationships are a vital part of our lives. Even more so when we face difficulties. God wants us to first seek Him and His strength. The more you study the Bible, the more you will realize God wants us to totally rely on Him for everything. We know through the verses above we should also seek the help of prayer warriors. In these passages of the Bible, God has given us the example and importance of prayer warriors, people who pray with and for us for a specific purpose.

Qualities of a Good Prayer Warrior

You want to be discerning as you seek your prayer warriors. They need to…

- Know the Bible well
- Understand the principles of prayer
- Be trustworthy
- Know how to keep a confidence and are not gossipers
- Be of the same gender as you. These are people you will have contact with on a regular basis. You want to avoid the appearance of wrong-doing, and you do not want to put yourself or your warriors in a position that may compromise their own

53

marriage. Emotions run high in times of trauma.

- Be someone you already know (preferably)
- Be calm and self-controlled. Your emotions may be on a roller coaster. You need the steadying influence of your warriors, not someone who is going to get emotional or hysterical over the situation.
- Be able and willing to commit time daily to pray for you and your family.

Ideally two or three prayer warriors are best, and within that group one is a confidante. Your pastor or counselor may also serve as a confidante though his or her time is less flexible than having a friend you can talk with when the need arises. I am so grateful I had a friend to teach me the importance of prayer warriors. She was a fountain of godly wisdom. In the midst of my difficulties, I drew strength from her confidence in God.

Prayer warriors are one part of our support network. Family and friends are traditionally members, though we rarely think of them in this manner. Within this group, we know to whom we can turn when we need help.

How does one establish a network?

Building a support system is a deliberate act of seeking out and developing positive relationships that model what we desire to be. Like a football coach seeks out a quarterback, we should be just as deliberate about whom we seek for our support system. If your goal is to be a strong, confident woman, befriend women who model that behavior and let them know you'd like their help.

You may be inclined to rely on one person, but this is an unhealthy option for you and your friend. No one can be there all the time and even our best friend can let us down occasionally — remember Peter, James, and John fell asleep. To revisit our football analogy, there are eleven men to each team, not just the coach and the quarterback. In addition, there are plenty of men on the sidelines ready to step in at any moment. Each man has specific skills he contributes to help the team win.

Your support system functions in much the same way, so incorporate a variety of people in your network. When I am feeling discouraged about my lack of career success, I talk with writer friends who understand the obstacles a freelance writer faces. When I'm feeling down, I talk with a friend I trust to give me godly encouragement and pray with me. I also include professionals, such as a counselor, in my network.

As the old adage goes "to make a friend, you have to be a friend." You also must be willing to offer support to your support network. As your relationship develops, you will each learn what you have to give and how you can support one another. Maybe your friend just needs someone to listen while she works through a problem; at other times it may be to walk the dog while your friend is laid up with a broken leg. These may seem like minor things, but they are all part of being there to help when help is needed, crisis or not.

I once had to place a loved one on a ninety-six-hour suicide watch. After leaving the hospital's mental health unit, but before I left the hospital parking lot, I activated another part of my support system. I called my church's prayer hotline and asked for prayer. I ask others to pray on my behalf because in Matthew 18:19, Jesus encourages me with these words, "I also tell you this: If two of you agree here on earth concerning anything you ask, my Father in heaven will do it for you."

I never hesitate to seek my most important teammate: God. The Bible tells me if I need wisdom, to ask our generous God, and He will give it to me. (See James 1:5). Perhaps it is part of our human nature, but all to often, we do everything we know to do to fix a problem and turn to God only after all our attempts fail. Asking for God's help should be the first thing we do. With His guidance we won't waste time on solutions that won't work. Additionally, with God's help comes His peace. (See Isaiah 26:3)

Today, my network includes many people beyond my family — friends, coworkers, my church family, and professionals. Establishing a resilient support network takes time. Don't worry, you have more of a support system than you may realize. For a helpful worksheet by Will Baum, LCSW, for developing a support network visit www.willbaum.com/wp-content/uploads/2009/12/My-Support-System-_Today-and-In-the-Future_.pdf.

If you attend church regularly, seeking help from your church family comes naturally. However, there are mothers in this situation who have told me they received negative reactions so much so that it was better for them to leave their church and find a new church home.

I cringe when I hear this. It puts Christians in a position of hypocrisy, judgment, and legalism. As it says in Romans 3:23, all have sinned. Only Jesus kept the Ten Commandments perfectly. Unfortunately, there are bodies of believers who rival the Pharisees in their hypocrisy and legalism.

If you sought help from your pastor and he stated he feels unqualified to counsel you, ask if he can recommend a pastor or does he know of a local church that offers counseling services. If not, make some phone calls of your own.

If you feel awkward or shunned by church friends (not the general church membership you are unacquainted with), examine that feeling. Are your own feelings of shame casting a shadow over your relationships? Do these friends know what is happening in your life? If not, it is likely your own emotions color the situation. If they do know, speak with them privately and tell them how you feel. Maybe they are uncomfortable around you because they just don't know what to say or do. They may be unaware of how their behavior is affecting you.

Even if unconsciously, believers and unbelievers expect Christians to behave differently. To be shunned or judged by church friends is hurtful. You expected understanding and encouragement, but got betrayal instead. Give the situation some time and seek God's guidance before seeking another church home.

God is always with you, sitting right next to you in the lead car of that roller coaster. The Bible is rich in promises and God is a promise keeper. (See Hebrews 10:23) Believe, and ask for help. He will supply you with His strength and power each day for every climb, descent, and turn life takes.

ACTION STEPS

• Seek out at least two women friends who are strong Christians knowledgeable in the Bible. Ask if they would be willing to pray for you on a daily basis and be available to advise and encourage you when needed. If you don't know anyone like this, talk with your pastor. He or she should be able to give you several names of women in the church who can help. Ask God's guidance as you seek help and for Him to bring the perfect prayer warriors.

• Evaluate your support system. What family, friends, and professionals do you know now that you can ask for help?

• During your prayer time, draw close to God and resist the devil. (See James 4:7-8)

• Ask God each day, every moment of the day if need be, to give you strength, wisdom, and guidance for the day. Seek Him first in all you do.

PRAYER

Father, as I draw near to You, draw near to me. My trust in You gives me freedom from my fear and worry because You supply all my needs. I seek your wisdom and guidance. Bring hope and healing into our lives. Guide me to prayer warriors who know the Bible from cover to cover and who can encourage me during this battle. In Jesus' name, amen. *(James 4:7-8, Psalm 23:1, Philippians 4:19)*

"For You have rescued me from my troubles and helped me to triumph over my enemies." — Psalm 54:7

CHAPTER 9

Easing Your Heartache

*"I will praise the LORD at all times. I will
constantly speak His praises." — Psalm 34:1*

MY STORY

In the course of six months my daughter had attempted suicide and been admitted to a psychiatric hospital; my husband had been arrested, convicted, and imprisoned; a fire burned our basement; and my oldest son was also arrested and jailed for sexually abusing his sister.

I felt as though I'd been hit by a train, body parts scattered everywhere, and left on the tracks to die, the passersby gawking and mocking me. Heartache pierced the depths of my soul.

REFLECTION

In this sinful world, hurt and broken hearts are a fact of life. God sees the depth of your hurt, and He hurts with you.

Every day I reminded myself of God's promise to make all things work for my good. What good could come from this mess, I didn't know, but I knew God would be faithful to His promise. I trusted His grace to carry me through my heartache and to heal each of us.

From the foundation of the earth, God provided for our comfort and healing. The Bible tells us in Isaiah 61:1-3 that

Jesus came to heal the brokenhearted, and to comfort and console those who mourn. It further states He gives us the garment of praise for our heaviness of spirit.

To praise is to express approval or admiration, and to worship is to render reverent honor and homage. Praise is an intentional act. When I praise God, He wraps me in a garment of His love, comfort, and peace.

Let's examine the power of praise with the example of Paul and Silas. In Acts 16:16-40 we find them in Philippi. Paul has cast out a demon of divination (fortune telling) from a slave girl. Her masters are angry because they can no longer profit from her fortune telling. They seize Paul and Silas and drag them to the authorities. The legal authorities of that day have Paul and Silas beaten with rods, thrown into prison, and their feet placed in stocks.

Our flesh would tell us to moan and cry and lash out at God if He put us in a similar situation. What did Paul and Silas do? Did they moan? Were they angry?

"Around midnight Paul and Silas were praying and singing hymns to God, and the other prisoners were listening." (Acts 16:25)

What happened next?

"Suddenly there was a massive earthquake, and the prison was shaken to its foundations. All the doors immediately flew open, and the chains of *every* prisoner fell off." (verse 26, author's emphasis). Everyone's chains fell off, not just those of Paul and Silas. Then the jailer tended to Paul's and Silas' wounds; Paul spoke to the jailer about Jesus; the jailer believed, and he and his family were baptized. That's the power of praise!

My experiences have taught me that praising God chases away my depression and soothes my broken heart. The most important time to praise God is when you're feeling your worst — so, no, you won't feel like praising. Praising God through your tears is a sacrifice, an exercise of your willpower. (See Hebrews 13:15) Your emotions scream at you to sit down and cry, but you must do your best to ignore your emotions and praise despite your tears. Don't hesitate to let the tears flow as you praise God.

Praise shifts your focus from your problems and puts it on God's power and promises. Praise fills your spirit with God's joy and peace. (See Nehemiah 8:10) When I praise God, my emotional state improves and my hope in God — my confident expectation that He'll do what He says He'll do — is restored. The gloom of my problems disappears. I can be still and listen for God's voice. That's not to say that this isn't difficult. Praising God in the midst of your heartache seems counter-intuitive. The first several times I did it, I had to gulp down my tears. Sometimes I finished my quiet time feeling better, sometimes I didn't. But the more I sought God in my down moments, the more it helped.

I've read through the Book of Psalms more times than I can count. A psalm is a sacred worship song. The psalmists express their deepest pains and anger at their enemies. They wonder where God is and why He allows their enemies to prosper. They do not hold back their emotions. In all but one psalm, they come to a point of once again praising God.

Doesn't it thrill you when your children spontaneously say "I love you"? God feels that way too, only infinitely more. Don't limit your praise to the praise and worship portion of Sunday church. Praise isn't just singing hymns. You are praising God when you state simply, "God, You are great and mighty." Praise God whenever and wherever you want — while standing in line at the grocery store (it doesn't have to be said out loud) or stopped at a red light, while you cook dinner or lie in bed at night unable to sleep.

Praise is a healing salve to your heartache. Let the power of God act on your behalf to ease your pain. The more you praise the more you will grow in confidence that God is in control and that what He allows in your life is what is best for you.

When we are in the middle of a crisis, it is difficult for us to envision how God can make good come from all the bad. I am a stronger person today than I might ever have been and He has inspired me to write this book so others can be helped through my experience. My daughter has earned a bachelor's degree in psychology and plans to earn a doctorate. Her ultimate goal is to counsel children who have been sexually abused.

ACTION STEPS

• If depression plagues you, lasting more than a week or two and interfering with your ability to function normally each day, seek professional help.

• Tune into a Christian radio station or put on some praise and worship music and sing along. Do your best to put your problems aside and focus on praising God for several minutes.

• If you don't have music, just talk to Him. I'll get you started.

PRAYER

Father, You are great and mighty and worthy to be praised. You deserve all glory and honor and blessing. How wonderful is the world You created for me. You are my refuge and my strength. I trust in You. You are omnipotent and omniscient. I love you. I love you, Jesus. I love you, Holy Spirit. I will praise You when I'm happy and when I'm sad. I will praise you in the good and in the bad. Your praise shall continually be in my mouth. (Now continue on your own.)

"Enter His gates with thanksgiving; go into His courts with praise." — Psalm 100:4

CHAPTER 10

Seek Professional Counsel

"Blessed is the man Who walks not in the counsel of the ungodly." — Psalm 1:1 (NKJV)

MY STORY

Withdrawn into myself like a snail into its shell, I sat in my counselor's office reading a detailed letter of all my husband had done to my daughter. His words devastated me.

During the court martial my husband admitted to three separate incidents. The truth he now revealed — he molested my daughter on a regular basis for nine years, even during the year we dated.

At this point, two years had elapsed since my daughter first came to me about her step-dad's inappropriate touches. During those two years, crisis after crisis ripped its way through our household. It took all my emotional and physical energy to deal with each situation and still keep the household running, but my wounds had begun to heal.

Now this letter stabbed at my heart afresh and ripped my tender heart wide open all over again. For the first time in my life I understood the anguish that drives a person to drink or take drugs or to murder. I sobbed for several minutes, then my counselor talked me through it.

REFLECTION

Foundational to a perpetrator's behavior are control and manipulation, and that extends to you and each of your children. I can't stress enough that your whole family can be affected by this abuse, especially if the abuser is a family member.

Within three months of my daughter's admission to the psychiatric hospital our family entered a counseling program designed for the whole family. My husband, my daughter, and I met regularly with our own therapists. These three counselors worked together in the same firm and conferred on our progress or lack thereof.

I can't imagine how I would have learned and healed and managed all I did if it hadn't been for my counselor. (I wonder if they own stock in Kleenex. They must go through more tissue than an elementary classroom of thirty students during peak cold and flu season.)

Finding quality counselors is essential. Finding someone who specializes in sexual abuse treatment is even better. The counseling group we used was not specifically Christian, but they knew we were and integrated Christian principles into our therapy sessions. It was an added benefit to be able to talk about my faith, how God was helping me through my difficulties, and to pray with my counselor at the end of each session.

I learned the thought processes and problems that contributed to my husband's crime. I learned the steps he would go through in his treatment. I learned how he manipulated me in order to get to my daughter. I also learned how my own behavior had become codependent, exacerbating the problems in our marriage.

Codependency defined in *Webster's Collegiate Dictionary* is "a psychological condition or a relationship in which a person is controlled or manipulated by another who is affected with a pathological condition (as an addiction to alcohol or heroine)."[1] In layman's terms, codependency is a relationship in which one person is addicted, either physically or psychologically, as in alcoholism, and the other person in the relationship is psychologically dependent on the first for his or her own well-being.

When social workers first spoke the word "codependency" during court hearings, I was outraged. For months I refused to believe that about myself. I considered myself an independent individual who didn't need to depend on anyone for safety, self-worth, or identity. Once I began to understand the true meaning of codependency and its intricacies, I began to see how my behavior had become just that. Like a cancer, codependency had invisibly invaded my life.

My husband had an addiction to sex. Of course I didn't know that when I met and married him. Within the first year of marriage, I recognized his obsession with perfection. The grass had to be just so green. The car had to glitter with cleanliness. The philodendron vines had to hang symmetrically from the planters. And when he came home from work all the toys had to be picked up off the floor and dinner ready, even though he often returned from work at various times.

He manipulated me by withholding his love, and manipulated my children through his outbursts of anger. I feared his rejection — a symptom of codependency — and tried my hardest to do what he expected. My own insecurities from childhood, carried into my life as an adult, probably made me predisposed or preconditioned to becoming codependent. The healthy response on my part would have been to assertively communicate with him the impossibility and irrationality of his demands.

There is a lot of disagreement in the mental health profession about codependency, whether it is or isn't an aspect of relationships that needs to change. My purpose in mentioning it is to help you realize that if your spouse is the perpetrator you may have unconsciously adopted unhealthy behaviors in order to adapt to your spouse's expectations.

I recommend you get counseling for yourself, not just for your daughter. She and your other children, if you have any, need you to be healthy in mind as well as body.

Be alert to the behavior of your other children. If they begin to act out or revert to childhood issues such as bed-wetting or thumb sucking, a deeper issue is involved. Professional help may be needed.

In addition to therapy, I sought the counsel of God, my prayer warriors, and pastor. Proverbs 11:14 says, "Where there is no counsel, the people fall; But in the multitude of counselors there is safety."

ACTION STEPS

• At a minimum, hire a professional counselor for your daughter. Ideally, one for yourself as well, no matter who committed the crime against your daughter.

• If you don't have insurance coverage, ask about a sliding fee or low-cost options. If you live near a medical teaching university, give them a call. They often have inexpensive programs.

• Don't let your fear of the cost stop you from getting the help you and your child need.

To find a counselor:
• Ask friends for referrals.
• Ask your pastor if he or she knows one they can recommend.

Other resources that can help you find a counselor:

• Focus on the Family, www.focusonthefamily.com, phone: 800-A-FAMILY, can offer referrals to local counselors as well as pray with you.

• Mental Health America, www.nmha.org, offers a wealth of information as well as aid in finding counselors in your area.

• The Department of Social Services

• The Yellow Pages under Mental Health may offer some viable options too.

• Interview each counselor over the phone. Then choose one and start. For specific questions to ask as you interview a counselor, turn to Appendix C.

PRAYER

Lord, thank You for today. Thank You for being with me every moment of the day to comfort me, lead me, and guide me. Guide me to the counselor you have designed for us, a counselor who specializes in child sexual abuse. Thank You for the work You have done in our lives already. In Jesus' name, amen.

(If you want a counselor who is a strong Christian and willing to use Christian principles during treatment, then be that specific in your prayers.)

"I will bless the LORD who has given me counsel." — Psalm 16:7 (NKJV)

CHAPTER 11

Recognize False Guilt

"But the LORD redeems those who serve Him. No one who takes refuge in Him will be condemned." — Psalm 34:22

MY STORY

I would never do anything to hurt Jenny," my husband told me the first year we were married. In one simple sentence he blinded me from seeing his wrong moves and manipulated me into blaming myself for what happened. Eight years later I sat across from my daughter. Both of us in tears.

"Mom, you were supposed to protect me," she said. But how could I protect her from something I didn't know was happening? Guilt and shame became my daily companions.

REFLECTION

Guilt and shame made me feel sullied. I cringe at the thought of how my daughter must have felt. Whenever I was out in public to run errands or attend church, I felt as though I wore a big sign that read: My husband is guilty of incest. But I didn't want anyone to know. Nearly three months passed before I told anyone in my extended family what was happening. Aside from the law, only two people outside my immediate family knew what was happening.

My husband made the choice to do what he did. (So did

your husband or whoever the perpetrator is.) But I carried guilt around for a long time. After all, I married the man who hurt my daughter and I failed to protect her.

In both cases, I experienced false guilt: guilt that is derived from misconceptions or feelings gone astray. True guilt is felt when biblical or moral beliefs are violated, such as stealing.

To convict is to prove guilty of an offense. To condemn is to pronounce censure or strong disapproval. The Holy Spirit uses conviction to make us aware of our true guilt. Satan (and others) uses condemnation to make us feel guilty about something of which we are innocent.

How can you tell the difference?

Conviction leads us to acknowledge wrong behavior, then to turn away from it and adopt healthy behavior in its place (much like an alcoholic states he is alcoholic and stops drinking). Condemnation leads nowhere positive. We continue to feel bad or guilty rather than led to make a healthy change. Yes, I married the man who then abused my daughter, but marriage isn't sinful. Yes, I failed to protect my daughter, but I took action to change things once I knew. If you're feeling condemnation, you are most likely experiencing false guilt.

In all situations that confront us, we have a choice whether to act or react. Reacting is allowing our emotions to control us; we respond without thinking. When we act, rather than react, we take control of our emotions and stop to think before we respond. We can't control everything that comes into our lives, but we can control our response to it.

When I learned the difference between true guilt and false, I was able to rethink my situation and discover the false guilt I carried around. This enabled me to discover the truth, which brings me to another important concept.

An old axiom states "actions speak louder than words." This

is no trite saying. It is truth. You probably think of it in relation to how others act toward you. Your husband says he loves you, but his action in abusing your daughter proves otherwise.

I want you to think about this in relation to your own words and actions. Do your actions line up with what you say? Do you say you're not fearful about your daughter's healing, but worry everyday about whether she'll lead an emotionally healthy adulthood? If so, that shows you believe something other than what you are saying. To carry this one step further, what you believe drives your actions.

Let me give you an illustration from my life. As a child I was extremely skinny — in an era when skinny wasn't popular, the 1950s and '60s. Doctor visits were frequent, but I felt fine. My peers daily ridiculed me. In my childhood immaturity, I embraced the belief that there was something wrong with me as a person. That I was unlovable and unlikable. As an adult I said what others thought of me wasn't important. But the underlying belief that I was somehow inferior drove me to perfectionist performance. My belief controlled my actions.

What we believe drives our actions, and those actions speak volumes over anything we might say. Stop and put the book down for a moment, and let that sink deep within you.

Therefore, it is critical to determine if what we believe is true or false.

In order to determine truth, we must have a standard by which to evaluate our beliefs. I once used societal norms, comparing myself with someone else's image or performance. As my experience with skinniness attests to, societal norms change with the regularity of the ocean's tide.

Then, I turned to the Bible. As a Christian this is the only source manual I should use to judge my beliefs about myself. The most valuable lesson I learned as I sought God's truth is that no matter what I do — right or wrong, fail or succeed — God will always love me. I'm sure I'll do something that disappoints Him — I'm extremely flawed — but He continues to love me anyway. What parent stops loving his or her child?

What does this have to do with false guilt? Many of the false beliefs I carried into adulthood predisposed me to my husband's manipulation. They also made it easier for me to embrace false guilt.

I'm a very introspective person, more so than most (and my therapist agrees). I often ask myself why I do what I do, why I believe what I believe. I've read a library full of self-help books to overcome the issues in my life. The advice in those books is intended to lead the way to change. But — and I'm going to be bold here — I believe permanent change is impossible if you hold false beliefs about the issue at hand.

That's why it's important to discover what you believe. Then you can replace false beliefs with the truth.

It's like erasing your answer on a true-false question in school. But don't confuse simple with easy. Erasing that answer took a few quick swipes of the eraser, but instilling truth into your psyche can be much more time consuming and difficult. With God's help it is possible.

Maybe this isn't where you are. But if you believe what happened to your daughter was your fault, you are releasing the perpetrator from his responsibility in the abuse. If you knew the abuse was happening and did nothing, you do share in the responsibility. However, if you knew nothing, you are not at fault. As I have stated previously, manipulation is common practice for a sexual abuser. It's how he gets what he wants and stops his victim from telling. My husband manipulated me, just as he did my daughter, and blinded me to what he was doing. Your husband (or whoever the perpetrator is) did the same to you.

This book is not intended to take the place of professional psychological help. It is intended to lead you down the road to healing and forgiveness by helping you build a strong foundation of who you are — a woman of God striving to be the best parent you can be. You are learning to recognize false guilt and false beliefs and replace them with truth. The truth will give you the confidence you need as you walk beside your daughter down the road to her own healing.

ACTION STEPS

- As you end your quiet time today, journal what you are feeling.
- Write down anything about which you may be feeling guilty and carefully examine it. Is it true guilt or false?
- If condemnation is ravaging you and you can't seem to take back control, memorize Romans 8:1 and say it out loud several times a day: "So now there is no condemnation for those who belong to Christ Jesus."
- If your actions aren't lining up with what you say you believe, take some time to reflect and discover your deep beliefs. Journal about your actions. For example, ask yourself "why do I get angry when _____ [fill in the blank]?" Then sit quietly expectant for an answer. It may not come right away, but with persistence, you will find the answer. (In some cases, professional counseling may be necessary.) Once you discover your core beliefs, you can take action to replace false beliefs you hold about yourself, others, and God.

PRAYER

Heavenly Father, reveal any area where I am feeling false

guilt. Help me recognize the lie behind false guilt and replace it with Your truths. Help me see false guilt whenever it comes knocking and refuse to open the door. Help me discover false beliefs I hold, and help me replace them with Your truths. Your Word says I will know the truth and the truth will set me free. Show me Your truth, Lord. Thank You that You do not condemn me, but that You forgive me. In Jesus' name, amen. *(John 8:32)*

> *"Guide my steps by Your word, so I will*
> *not be overcome by evil." — Psalm 119:133*

CHAPTER 12

Stress Relief:
the Practical Aspects

"Show me where to walk, for I give
myself to You." — Psalm 143:8b

MY STORY

I prayed daily and thanked God for financial provision. I didn't have a job, but there were plenty of other things that devoured my time: trips to court, counseling, visiting my daughter at the hospital, and making trip after trip to stores to find carpet, paint, and furniture for the basement to replace what was lost in the fire. I would have lost my sanity for sure with the added stress of a job.

REFLECTION

Each situation is individual. As a stay-at-home mom I didn't have to juggle a job along with all the appointments civil court demanded of me. Counseling occurred during the day when I had the physical and mental (if not the emotional) energy to attend. But one crisis after another assaulted me. My stress level reached a new peak everyday. More than once I felt on the edge of a nervous breakdown. Stress relief became mandatory if I was to remain healthy and sane.

To help manage stress I learned relaxation techniques. I sought information on the Internet and asked my counselor for resources as well.

Here are a few relaxation benefits MayoClinic.com reports:

- Improves concentration
- Reduces anger and frustration
- Boosts confidence to handle problems[1]

Utilizing relaxation techniques on a regular basis will help you de-stress. You may feel finding time for one more thing is too much, but I'm not suggesting a thirty-minute period of time. Even five minutes of relaxation will help. You can do it when you lie down to sleep for the night. You can even learn to relax on your drive home from work each day. To learn more, read this article on stress reduction from Mayo Clinic: www.mayoclinic.org/healthy-living/stress-management/in-depth/relaxation-technique/art-20045368

If you do not already practice stress relief principles, start now. Stress attacks your immune system, making you more susceptible to illness. It is stressful enough to work full time and manage home and family when things are going well. A crisis obliterates your daily routine.

You won't be of any benefit to your family if you land in the hospital with a nervous breakdown or major illness. Below are several recommendations to counter the affects of stress on your body:

- Get at least eight hours of sleep every night. Sleep is designed to help the body and brain rejuvenate. The proper amount of sleep each night can be your #1 weapon against stress.

• Eat healthy and drink plenty of water.

• Take a quality multi-vitamin and mineral supplement. Make sure it contains the daily value of B-complex. B vitamins are essential to your nervous system and are often called the happy vitamins because they boost your mood. A cup of Tension Tamer herbal tea is nice now and then, too!

• Take a walk two to three times a week if you are not already in the habit of regular exercise.

• Do relaxation exercises at least once a week. (Google search to find ones that will work for you.)

All the extra appointments I had each month demanded my physical and emotional energy. When I came home, I often didn't want to face cooking a meal. Turning to fast food, or processed, instant boxed meals appealed to my tired body — and brain. I'm not a health-food enthusiast, but I do what I can to avoid meals straight from a box or can. These instant meals are high in sodium, preservatives, and other chemicals (and calories). Plus they are more expensive than buying the ingredients separately. When your income gets cut in half like ours did, you save dollars everywhere you can.

With a bit of planning, you can avoid the fast and instant food. Meal ideas:

• Plan two weeks (or even a month) of supper at a time. Write it on the calendar and make your grocery list accordingly. Just having it written down will free up some brain cells and chase away the frustration of "What am I going to fix for dinner tonight?". And you won't be making last minute trips to the grocery store because you decided at 4:30 to have reuben sandwiches for dinner, but didn't have any swiss cheese.

• Invest in a Crock Pot if you do not already own one. They

save time, energy, and added heat on those hot summer days. Toss your supper into the pot before the kids are up. Then it's done and off your mind (until the delicious aromas entice you), and you won't have hungry kids clamoring while you're trying to cook.

• When preparing supper, make a double portion. Freeze half to pull out on a busy day that catches you by surprise.

• Spend a Saturday cooking some of your favorite meals and putting them directly into the freezer. Search "once a month cooking" for sites that offer recipes and ideas for bulk meal plans and preparations. Make this a fun family activity by letting the kids get involved. Allow the kids to do age-appropriate tasks and choose some of the dishes and desserts you make.

• Use the many websites that offer free recipes. They add variety, ease, and value to your meals. If you're a Pinterest user, you already know of the abundance of recipes listed there.

• If friends notice you are going through a difficult time and ask what they can do to help, ask if they'll prepare a meal. Many of us find it hard to ask for help. Take a deep breath, and remember friends ask because they care and want to help. Smile and say something like, "Thank you so much. Could you prepare a meal I can put in the freezer for next week?"

These ideas are effective in saving you time and money, as well as keeping you nourished. The purpose is to make a busy day less harried while easing the financial strain of fast food restaurant meals.

Stress takes a toll on your thought processes as well. You likely have a number of new appointments — possibly including court hearings. Rather than try to remember them, make use of a daily calendar (like the ones you get free in the mail every year). Write those appointments down and refer to the calendar each morning as you begin your day. You will be less likely to be late for an appointment, or worse yet, miss it altogether because you forgot.

The added stress and heartache you feel can also place stress on your personal relationships. Know the priorities of the relationships in your life and how to maintain those relationships.

- I recommend you make your relationship with God the first priority. "[W]ith God all things are possible" (Matt. 19:26) and without Jesus "you can do nothing." (John 15:5c) He can and will sustain you. Pray and read the Bible daily. You can pray while showering, during your commute, washing dishes, etc. Any mundane task that doesn't require your concentration can be used for prayer time. God cared for me, and He'll do the same for you.
- Your family comes next — first your husband, then your children (in a healthy marriage). Do your best to be there for them when they need you. Eat meals together; spend time having fun; discuss their day and pray with your children as you put them to bed; consider having a family devotional time daily or weekly.
- Your job. It will help your supervisor understand your demeanor, attitude, and work efficiency by knowing your personal situation. If court or counseling appointments are pulling you away from work more than you can manage, your supervisor or someone in the human resources department of the company could suggest options that are available to you. Does this situation qualify for leave under the Family Medical Leave Act? Is part-time or flextime possible? How about a leave of absence? Keep an open mind. If you aren't comfortable with informing your supervisor, seek the advice of a trusted business friend or your pastor. Their objective perspectives will offer possibilities you may not think of.

A great stress reliever is laughter. "A cheerful heart is good medicine." (Proverbs 17:22) Yes, laughter is medicine, and it doesn't taste nasty going down either. Here are just a few of the benefits of laughter:

- Releases endorphins, the body's natural feel-good chemicals, into the body
- Relaxes the body
- Boosts the immune system
- Improves the function of blood vessels and increases blood flow.

I envy people who can stare down a crisis and stab it in the heart with a one-liner. My oldest son is a person like that. Usually his one-liners are quotes from a movie given in the actor's voice. He can do a fantastic Shaggy and Scooby routine. The most quoted line in our family is Sean Connery's line "Some things in here don't react well to bullets," from the movie *Hunt for Red October.* My daughter has an amazing sense of humor. I've often told her she should be a stand-up comic. Now me, I'm often accused of taking life too seriously. I agree. I've tried to change, but my sense of humor is so dry it rivals Death Valley. I actually like the smell of a skunk. What does that say about my personality?

Laughter reduces the levels of stress hormones and increases the happy hormones. It also helps you gain a better perspective of a negative situation. I'm not a humor writer, but I look for something to laugh about during a crisis, because if I don't, more than my sense of humor ends up in Death Valley. There are two good things about the endless stream of forwarded emails I get, (1) It tells me people are thinking about me. That's comforting; (2) They often provide a good belly laugh.

The Bible says, "And give thanks for everything to God the Father in the name of our Lord Jesus Christ." (Ephesians 5:20) Johnson Oatman, Jr. wrote the hymn "Count Your Blessings" and had it published in 1897. That was long before scientists studied the health benefits of giving thanks. Mr. Oatman didn't need scientists to confirm what he learned through experience — saying thank you regularly improves your state of mind. Today's scientists have also proven the activity has physical benefits as well. But you must say "thank you" more often than once a year to gain the benefits.

Offer thanksgiving even in the tough times. I know from experience that's hard. I don't necessarily thank God for sending tough times. I thank Him for being with me and giving me the strength to get through them.

ACTION STEPS

Take a moment and give your stress level an honest appraisal. Are you near the edge? Between what I've already discussed and the bulleted list below, pick out at least two items to help relieve your stress.

• Find some relaxation exercises that work for you and employ them daily.

• Has your daily routine taken a vacation? That's to be expected. Take a deep breath and tell yourself it's okay. Do what you can in small ways to re-establish your pre-crisis routine.

• Delegate new chores to your children, such as doing the laundry, watering plants, vacuuming, dusting, preparing a meal. Be sure the chores are age-appropriate.

• When friends offer help, accept it. Prepare a list with their names and phones numbers. Most people usually ask "what can I do?" so think ahead of time what you are comfortable with and prepare a second list. Could they babysit an hour or two and allow you to get away? Prepare a meal? Mow the grass? Take your kids to football practice? With this prepared list, you won't be caught off guard with nothing to say but "no, I'm fine."

• Are you getting enough laughter? Take time to have fun. Once or twice a month do something just for fun — get together with friends for games, hike, take the kids to the park, take in a movie, have coffee with friends, etc. Do what you find fun.

• Take time weekly or monthly to enjoy a hobby. Hobbies are great stress relievers. Practically anything you enjoy doing can be made into a hobby.

• Know what rejuvenates your physical and emotional energy and make time for it. I need alone time. Others need the companionship of friends. Learn to recognize the things that energize you and include them in your life on a regular basis.

• Give thanks to God when you wake up and when you go to bed.

PRAYER

Heavenly Father, You know all I have to handle. Give me the strength and stamina I need for work and home. Help me find rest and balance in the midst of this situation. Show me any tasks I can give up to lessen my load. Help me find techniques that will relax me and relieve my stress. Thank You for the Bible, which gives me strength, encouragement, comfort, and guidance. You know my needs before I ever express them; You are my provider. Thank You for providing. In Jesus' name, amen.

"In peace I will lie down and sleep, for You
alone, O LORD, will keep me safe." — Psalm 4:8

CHAPTER 13

Stress Relief: the Emotional Aspect

"Why am I discouraged? Why is my heart so sad?
I will put my hope in God!" — Psalm 42:5

MY STORY

Mental numbness from the stress obliterated every celebration that first year. My daughter celebrated her thirteenth birthday in the psychiatric hospital. I think I took her a homemade cupcake. My two sons also celebrated birthdays three months into this family crisis. Did I bake birthday cakes and buy presents? Did I fix turkey and all the trimmings for Thanksgiving and Christmas dinner? What Christmas presents did I buy? Who put up the tree? A few pictures exist to testify we observed Christmas, but my memory is a blank page. The trauma of the crises of the previous four months had my brain on overload.

REFLECTION

As tempting as it was at times, it was important for me not to rely on my kids to fulfill my responsibilities. I was the parent, and they needed me to be the parent. I did my best to keep my tears hidden. I discussed my frustrations with a friend and kept the pity parties private (and there were plenty of them).

My children were going through an upheaval in life just as I was. Their step-dad had been removed from the house by armed military police and later court-martialed and sent to prison. Their sister spent three months in a psychiatric hospital, and my two sons barely escaped the fire that gutted the basement.

I was the one constant in their lives. They needed me to re-establish stability in our home.

My children received counseling, but they still acted out. My daughter ran away from home so many times I lost count. She was in and out of foster homes, and at the age of fifteen had a baby. Those are crisis-level events added to an already heaping pile. The trauma and stress of it obliterated portions of my memory as I related above. I battled for three years before I came to a point where God took me from His arms of grace and set my feet back on the ground. Yes, there were good times. I trusted the Lord to bring us through to the other side and He did. "I would have lost heart, unless I had believed That I would see the goodness of the LORD In the land of the living." (Psalm 27:13 NKJV)

The stress of everything nearly overwhelmed me. I don't mean to scare you, but this crisis didn't resolve in one month or one year. Our instant society has conditioned us to expect everything quickly. Reality doesn't work that way. Understand this will more than likely take longer to resolve than you anticipate. Knowing that ahead of time will give you strength to face it if it happens. I pray your situation is not as intense as mine was, or lasts as long. God will carry you just as He carried me, in His loving arms of grace. Trust and believe.

The point I want to make here is I didn't lie in bed depressed over the situation and force my two oldest children, then ages thirteen and seventeen, to daily look after their three-year-old little brother and cook dinner and clean house. I don't say that to brag or put pressure on you, but to make you aware.

My kids still had their usual chores and responsibilities. Yes, they helped with watching their little brother while I was busy cleaning or cooking, etc. But they didn't assume the responsibility of running the house while I sat despondent and helpless. I worked to maintain our family routine and bring some normalcy to our day despite the troubles. I remained the parent, rather than allowing my children to slip into that role.

My husband's crime made our family a single-parent home overnight. That situation robbed not only my daughter, but each of my children of a portion of their childhood. Whatever the exact circumstances of your situation, don't allow your children's remaining childhood to be stolen by letting them become a parent to you.

I made the determination from the very beginning that my family would remain intact. I committed to do all I could do to help my children heal. I tackled one day at a time. You can too. I succeeded because I had God's help and His strength. With God, you will also succeed.

When incest struck my home, I was home schooling my two oldest and my youngest was still in diapers. My social life consisted of a women's weekly Bible study group. Everyone's needs came before mine. Even now as a mature woman of fifty-eight, I tend to neglect my needs. I feel selfish when I'm spending time pampering myself in some way, especially if it means I'm having fun without family members. But a healthy life is a balanced life. I must keep my body, mind, and spirit healthy. Taking care of me isn't the equivalent of living it up and leaving the family at home every weekend.

Psalm 37 (rendered here from the NKJV) is an ideal daily living guide and encourager.

Verse 1: "Do not fret." No amount of worry is going to make things better. It drags you down — body, mind, and spirit. "A fretful, discontented spirit is open to many temptations," says Matthew Henry in his *Concise Commentary on the Whole Bible.*[1] Worry means you don't trust God to take care of things.

Verse 3: "Trust in the LORD;... Dwell in the land and feed on His faithfulness." This is the answer to your worry. Trust in and believe God. You are a citizen of heaven and a child of God. All that He has is yours. Ask for what you need. He keeps you in His peace when you keep your thoughts fixed on Him. (See Isaiah 26:3)

Verse 4: "Delight yourself in the LORD." Praise and thank Him regularly. Rejoice in His love for you. This stops anger from gaining control and wards off depression. If feelings of depression persist every day for two weeks or more and impact your ability to function at home, at work, or socially, seek professional help.

Verse 5: "Commit your way to the LORD." To commit something is to entrust it to someone else's oversight. So to commit your way to the Lord is to trust that He brings only what's best into your life, that He'll guide your every footstep. (See Psalm 37:23, Psalm 32:8, and Proverbs 16:3) Give Him your concerns and your dreams, your life and your children's lives, give everything to God and trust Him to work.

Verse 7: "Rest in the LORD and wait patiently for Him." When you live the four steps mentioned above, the logical conclusion is to rest, believe you have received, and wait for God to act. As you pray, thank Him for the answers He is bringing to your prayers. Thankfulness for His answers will help you stay focused on God rather than on the problem.

Psalm 37 ends with a promise. "But the salvation of the righteous is from the LORD; He is their strength in the time of trouble. And the LORD shall help them and deliver them; He shall deliver them from the wicked, and save them, because they trust in Him." (verses 39, 40) Hallelujah! God not only gives us guidance on how to live, He also promises action on His part.

Let's extrapolate on that. If God failed to meet His promise, that would make Him a liar. If He is a liar, then He is imperfect and not God. Malachi 3:6 tells us God does not change. James 1:17 also tells us He never changes. If God failed to perform even one word of the Bible, that would make the whole Bible useless. If we are to believe in God, it is to believe He is perfect in every way: all-powerful, all-knowing, all-present, infinite, and immutable (not capable of change). What He says and promises we can trust Him to perform. (See Hebrews 10:23)

I didn't know all of this when life came crashing down around me. I learned most of it along the way. I hope by sharing it here, you can glean from my knowledge to make your journey smoother and a lot less stressful.

ACTION STEPS

- Take one day at time. Don't worry about tomorrow. (See Matthew 6:34)
- Continue as much as possible with the daily routine you had established before this happened.
- If you are struggling to stay focused, make a to-do list to remind you of the tasks for the day or keep a daily calendar.
- Above all, be there for your children. Listen to them, comfort them, discipline them, have fun with them.
- Trust God to guide you. Spend time with God at least three to four times/week (daily is even better) in prayer and reading the Bible.
- Just as you see to the needs of your family, be sure that

you see to your own.

- For further reading on stress and its effects, www.webmd.com/mental-health/effects-of-stress-on-your-body

PRAYER

Lord, thank You. Thank You for Your Word that gives me strength, encouragement, comfort, and guidance. Help me find rest and balance in the midst of chaos. In Jesus' name, amen.

"Be still in the presence of the LORD, and wait patiently for Him to act." — Psalm 37:7

CHAPTER 14

Just What Is Forgiveness?

"He will judge the world with justice and
rule the nations with fairness." — Psalm 9:8

MY STORY

What do you want from me?" my estranged husband yelled. It was yet another of our many arguments. He had abused my daughter and broken my heart beyond repair. I marveled that he could even ask such a question.

"I want you to hurt as much as I do," I told him.

REFLECTION

"I'll never forgive you!" I hear those words quite often on television shows and in movies. In reality, many struggle to forgive those who hurt them.

When someone hurts us, we hold that person accountable for his actions. He wounded us and must pay the price and suffer the consequences. Justice must be served. Deep down we want that person to hurt too!

Revenge is defined as: 1) to exact punishment or expiation for a wrong on behalf of, especially in a resentful or vindictive spirit; 2) to take vengeance for.[1]

The Bible clearly states that vengeance belongs to the Lord. (See Deuteronomy 32:35) Romans 12:19 tells us, "Dear friends, never take revenge. Leave that to the righteous anger of God. For the Scriptures say, 'I will take revenge; I will pay them back.' says the LORD."

As a Christian, I know God commands us to forgive. From the beginning I determined to forgive my husband for what he did to my daughter. But for months on end I struggled with it. I grew up with the cliché "forgive and forget." I thought to forgive also meant to forget and act as though nothing had ever happened. But something *had* happened, and I didn't want this man back in my life or my children's lives in any way. To forget was asking too much.

Like a ricocheting bullet, "forgive and forget" did its damage, forcing me to my knees time and again in an effort to forgive my husband. I pleaded with God to help me understand what forgiveness meant.

I studied the biblical passages on forgiveness and read other material I could find. I listened more attentively when my pastor spoke about forgiveness. When I heard someone on the radio or TV discuss the topic my ears were tuned in.

Then one night I heard a pastor speak specifically about "forgive and forget" and it set me free. When we have suffered some pain, be it physical or emotional, at the hands of someone else, we have a right to justice — that the perpetrator be punished for his crime. Forgiveness means you give up your right to demand punishment of the person who wronged you and allow God to handle it.

Please don't misunderstand me here. I'm not saying don't file charges if a crime has been committed. In fact, not to take legal action in the name of forgiveness is a terrible wrong against the victim of sexual abuse and your community as a whole. If an abuser isn't stopped, he/she will continue to abuse and hurt others. Allow the legal system to take action, then step back and trust God to exact justice.

God didn't expect me to forget, nor did He ask me to. Finally I had permission to not forget. That enabled me to fully commit to forgive my husband and concentrate on healing.

Emotionally I didn't feel like forgiving him (we rarely feel like forgiving). The usual objections paraded through my mind: What he did was unforgivable; he doesn't deserve to be forgiven. The thought of forgiving him left a nasty taste in my mouth, as disgusting as a mouthful of dirt.

I knew God's command to forgive (see Matthew 6:14-15), and I didn't want unforgiveness in my heart to hinder my relationship with God. With each passing day, with each ordeal, the criminal and civil court trials, there were new hurts. I had to remind myself regularly that I'd forgiven my husband, and I had to forgive the new hurts. My emotions rarely lined up with my decision, but God provided me with His grace and strength.

Through all this I learned forgiveness isn't a process. It's a decision, an act of the will. It isn't like dishing out a bowl of soup one spoonful at a time. Forgiveness is completed the moment we make the decision. My ex-husband isn't any more forgiven today than he was twenty years ago when I forgave him.

Forgiveness isn't…

- denying that a wrong occurred
- forgetting the wrong, or
- approving the wrong (saying "It's okay that you did this to me").

Additionally, forgiveness doesn't mean you have to allow that person into your life, especially if the relationship is unsafe.

Forgiveness is for our benefit, not the abuser's. An unforgiving heart is fertile ground for bitterness, and bitterness poisons our spirit. Proverbs 17:9 says, "Love prospers when a fault is forgiven." Forgiveness is a choice of our free will. We can demand justice and grow bitter, or forgive and find healing.

ACTION STEPS

- When you find thoughts of revenge seeping in, give them to God immediately. If you embrace these thoughts, they will work their way into your heart and bitterness will take root. It may very well lead you down a road that ends in jail. Thoughts you dwell on drive you to action; make those thoughts positive and productive.
- Forgiveness is a choice. The more horrific the wrong against you, the more difficult that choice is. You won't feel like forgiving, but with time, your emotions will line up with your choice. Persevere and give it time.
- Anger and thoughts of unforgiveness will taunt you. Each time they occur remind yourself you have forgiven this person already. Ask for God's help, for when we are weak, He is strong.
- Luke 6:28 tells us to pray for those who hurt us. That may seem impossible. Like forgiveness, doing this is also a choice. Several months past before I first prayed this way, but once I started I found it aided my healing. God is a God of mercy. He loves my ex-husband as much as He loves me. God grieved over this wrong, too. He desires each of us to be in relationship with Him, and for us to live in heaven with Him for eternity. When we pray for those who hurt us, we begin to see them from God's perspective.
- Be encouraged. Our forgiveness and healing is accomplished through God's power, rather than from our willpower. "So let us come boldly to the throne of our gracious God. There we will receive His mercy, and we will find grace to help

us when we need it most." (Hebrews 4:16) Go to God in prayer and ask for His help to forgive those who have wounded you, and to bring healing, physically, emotionally, and mentally.

PRAYER

Father, forgive me for my hate and anger. I want _____ (insert perpetrator's name) to be punished for what he's done to my daughter, but the Bible tells me vengeance belongs to You. I give _____ (name) over to You; You are his judge. I choose to forgive _____ (name). Help my emotions line up with my choices and help me to forgive. In Jesus' name, amen.

"But the LORD is in His holy Temple; the LORD still rules from heaven. He watches everyone closely, examining every person on earth." — *Psalm 11:4*

CHAPTER 15

Forgive Yourself

*"I am worn out from sobbing. All night I flood
my bed with weeping, drenching it with my tears.
My vision is blurred by grief . . ." — Psalm 6:6-7*

MY STORY

Failure besieged me regularly. I took special refuge in Psalms 37 and 91. Circumstances didn't improve as fast as I wanted them to. I felt I was failing my children as well as myself. I beat myself down with my words and thoughts. All the big and little failures of my forty-some years tramped across the stage of my mind.

REFLECTION

The effects of traumatic events leave wounds that can hide for years. Even when you think your wounds are healed, they can surprise you in an area totally unrelated to your trauma.

One morning the organization I worked for announced a reorganization, and we were told we would have to interview for the positions established in the new department. I panicked — inexplicably, unequivocally panicked.

Where was this panic coming from? I was clueless. I battled fear all evening; I slept very little. The next morning as I prayed during my thirty-minute drive to work, I broke down and cried. As soon as I got into the office, God led me to seek out a certain co-worker. Ensconced in a conference room with tissue in hand, we spoke for nearly forty-five minutes. This Christian woman, mature with insight and godly wisdom from her life's experiences, discerned I had not forgiven myself. (This same woman now has a full-time ministry of forgiveness). Just as important as forgiving those who wound us, we must also forgive ourselves for what we perceive as our shortcomings, mistakes, and failures.

My marriage had failed. My children were miserable. I viewed this as failure on my part. Perfection controlled me. I must be perfect; if I wasn't no one would accept me. Like falling dominoes, one realization led to another. Failure meant rejection, and rejection meant I was unlovable... and... and ... and. Layers of childhood and adult wounds infected my thought processes and obstructed rational responses.

The reason behind my unexplained panic? I believed if I lost my job, it would be yet another failure in my life — another potential loss in my life that someone else had control over. I trusted these people. They were dear friends who helped me find healing. My conscious mind fixated on failure, but my subconscious screamed BETRAYAL. (The mind is a complex thing.) Through all this, an important question I learned to ask myself is "Why am I acting like this?"

What we perceive becomes our reality. If we believe it is true, it becomes true for us. "For as he thinks in his heart, so is he." (Proverbs 23:7, NKJV). Remember, our actions demonstrate our beliefs. (See chapter 11, "Recognize False Guilt") An illustration of this principle is the anorexic who believes she is fat even when she is on the verge of dying of starvation. Everyone around her sees the truth, but the anorexic believes she is fat, and that belief then drives her actions.

Most of us tend to be our own worst critic. We demand standards of behavior we expect of no one else. No one is perfect, and we must come to terms with our mistakes and failures. Forgiving yourself is the first step.

ACTION STEPS

• Dedicate a portion of your quiet time to determine if there are things for which you haven't forgiven yourself. Make a list in your journal. Pray over each item and tell yourself "I forgive you."

• If you're behaving oddly and forgiveness isn't the issue, set aside some time to examine your behavior. Examine your feelings, thoughts, and expectations. Is fear attacking? Are you demanding perfection from yourself or others? Ask yourself the necessary questions to dig deep into why you're behaving the way you are. Try to determine the cause and address it. Ask a trusted friend for their insight or seek professional help if needed.

• Reread the chapter "Recognize False Guilt" and replace false beliefs with the truth where necessary.

PRAYER

Father, help me to forgive myself and others. Reveal false perceptions I have about myself and my life. Help me see myself as You see me — Your child, beautiful and capable, and full of potential. In Jesus' name, amen.

"O Lord, You are so good, so ready to forgive, so full of unfailing love for all who ask for Your help." — Psalm 86:5

CHAPTER 16

Healing Your Daughter's Heart

"Weeping may last through the night,
but joy comes with the morning." — Psalm 30:5

MY STORY

From my daughter's perspective, I had betrayed her because I failed to protect her. She expressed her anger at me through disobedient behavior, running away, and arguments too often to number. It seemed to me her anger toward me was more pronounced and deep than her anger with her step-dad for abusing her.

REFLECTION

A child expects her parents to protect her. Incest destroys that protection. Daddy, the man who is supposed to love and protect her, has instead, violated and controlled her in horrifying ways. Now she seeks to protect herself and exert control whenever and wherever she can.

Your daughter is hurting, and hurting people often protect themselves by hurting first — a preemptive strike, if you will. The thinking goes something like this: I've been hurt; I'm not going to get hurt again; therefore, I'll hurt you before you can hurt me.

When your daughter is pushing your buttons, step back, take a deep breath, and pause for a moment. Remember she is hurting and doesn't want to get hurt again. This will give you a healthier, objective perspective on the situation. You will be less inclined to take your daughter's actions personally. This moment of thought can help you respond calmly to enforce the rules with love.

Confrontation between parent and child happens even in healthy families. A child pushes the limits. She thinks she is testing how much she can get away with, but she is actually discovering how much you care about her and her safety. A child needs and wants security. She wants to know a boundary exists and that you will enforce it. It is important you establish and maintain the house rules and allow the natural (or established) consequences to take place when the rules are broken.

As your child grows, you give her opportunities to learn self-control through choices. As she enters her teen years, she is going to want to take control of all her choices. This isn't always easy for parents to handle, and it doesn't mean there are no rules or expectations. The more you attempt to control a child or teen's behavior, the more control you'll lose. A tighter grip actually pushes teens away and ripens your home environment for control battles. As parents, we must learn to let go and let our children grow up.

Depending on the age of your child, you may face varied behavioral issues. This is one of many reasons why counseling for yourself is as essential as it is for your daughter. The counselor has insight on those issues and how best to handle them.

When your daughter makes you angry, she may not realize or even understand for herself why she's doing it. She's hurting; she wants to get a reaction from you; she wants to get her way about something. The reasons are too numerous to list. Do your best to not take her words and actions as a personal assault against you. That's not to say what is said and done won't hurt. Try to respond calmly rather than defensively or offensively. "Most important of all, continue to show deep love for each other, for love covers a multitude of sins." (1 Peter 4:8)

In a private moment, make a note of the positive and negative behaviors you notice each day. Yes, even the positive ones. They can be a sign of growth, but also an unhealthy coping mechanism. Take this list to your counseling appointment so you won't struggle to remember an issue you wanted to discuss.

Unconditional love doesn't come naturally. And you may not even realize you are placing conditions on your love. When you display love toward your child only when he or she behaves the way you want, that is conditional love. When you must discipline your child, stay calm and speak without anger in your voice. Explain what he or she did wrong, and state it was the behavior you disapprove of, then reassure your child of your love.

In my days as a young parent, I made a lot of mistakes, fueled by my own insecurities. I did my best, but I learned better parenting techniques way too late for them to help my daughter and me. By then, my daughter's behavior was completely out of my control. Civil court placed specific requirements on me that I worked to maintain, but about which my daughter knew nothing. She thought I was being controlling just because.

In her hurt, my daughter did many things to push me away, crushing the broken and still bleeding pieces of my heart. She knew all the right buttons to push and our relationship had more slow climbs and sudden drops than a super roller coaster. I had to remind myself that my daughter was dealing with our situation from the maturity level of a young teen despite her appearance and behavior that screamed "I want to be treated as an adult." Part of the time I responded rationally and assertively, and other times I reacted from the depth of my hurt.

At times her behavior presented an unhealthy, unsafe environment for my toddler and me. She bounced between my house and foster homes for three years. At the age of 15, she had a baby, and at 16, moved permanently to foster care at her request. In all honesty, I felt relieved. I know that sounds terrible, perhaps even heartless. Our constant arguing kept our household in turmoil, our stress levels on overload, and our pain raw. The time apart allowed our wounds to heal and kept us from inflicting new ones.

As my daughter neared the age of eighteen, I knew the Department of Social Services would soon release her from foster care. She would be on her own, working to forge the kind of life she wanted for herself. Would that life include me? Our relationship was strained at best — almost nonexistent. Time had healed only a few of our wounds. It seemed no matter how much prayer and effort I put into making things better, a wall of pain still divided us.

My heart ached over our broken relationship. When would God bring reconciliation and restoration? From my front deck one afternoon, I looked out at Pikes Peak as if expecting God to speak to me from the mountain as He had to Moses on Mount Sinai. God, what should I do?

Apologize.

My pride bristled at what I sensed God telling me. What had I done wrong that I should apologize? I was being the best parent I knew how to be. Still, I felt like such a colossal failure. Admitting another mistake would seal the deal. Deep down I knew I had failed her. When she needed me most, I wasn't there to stop her step-father from hurting her.

I didn't trust myself to say the right words over the phone, so I grabbed a piece of paper and a pencil and wrote a letter.

"Dear Jenny, I'm sorry I wasn't there to protect you. Please forgive me." For the first time in a long time, I felt at peace.

A few days later, the phone rang. "Mom, I got your letter."

I held my breath, expecting an argument to ensue as it so often did. We talked at length and before the conversation was over we were both crying. God had opened the door to restoration.

If I had not set my pride aside and asked my daughter to forgive me, our relationship may have never healed. At best, it would have taken years longer for the door to open. Forgiveness allowed healing and restoration of the relationship to occur.

Our relationship followed a rocky road for many years, which I took one day at a time. Today, twenty years after it all began, my daughter and I are as close as any mother and daughter can be. Perhaps closer because of the struggles we have shared and overcome.

God loves us unconditionally. No matter what hurtful thing we do to Him or to others, He continues to love us. And when we ask Him to forgive us, He does.

If we expect people who hurt us to say "I'm sorry," then we must be willing to do the same. Next to "I love you," the most important words we can speak to the people in our lives are "Please forgive me."

ACTION STEPS

- Love your daughter unconditionally. Pray for the ability to love your daughter as God loves her.
- Stay calm in the midst of angry confrontations. Defuse the moment by remaining calm and loving in your response. Think before you speak and don't allow your emotions to control you. Be assertive. (I realize that's easier said than done!) Is she simply misbehaving or acting out?

- Do not give up on your relationship. Persist and pray for your daughter daily. If needed, pray for restoration to your relationship.

- Read the age-appropriate *Parenting with Love and Logic* book or other parenting books your counselor may recommend.

- Ask God for insight and discuss with your counselor those actions or situations that trigger your anger. Formulate possible responses for the next occurrence.

- Establish boundaries for your relationship and don't violate them or allow your daughter to either.

- Allow your daughter the age-appropriate level of choices and control.

- Listen closely to what your daughter is trying to tell you and talk through her complaints. If she isn't talking, observe her behavior closely for warning signs (cutting, substance abuse, eating disorders) of more serious issues. Ask your counselor for guidance in this area.

- Allow your daughter to heal from her wounds and mature. As she matures, she will gain a new perspective that will allow her to re-evaluate her childhood perceptions.

- Seek the advice of your counselor or pastor when needed.

- Do not consider yourself a failure at parenting if your daughter goes to foster care. Concentrate on getting emotionally healthy and providing a healthy home for your other children. This time apart will give your daughter-inflicted wounds a chance to heal.

- Whether your daughter is placed in foster care or not, place her care in God's hands. Allow God to work in her life and bring healing to her wounds.

PRAYER

(As you pray this prayer, if necessary replace the word "her" with "him.")

Father, You are great and mighty and worthy to be praised. Forgive my anger. Help me to understand why I get angry, and instead of responding in anger, help me to respond with unconditional love. When _____ (child's name) hurts me, help me to just keep loving.

I place _____ (child's name) in Your hands. Cradle her in Your loving arms. Let her know and feel the deep love You have for her, and that You are there to carry her through this ordeal. Be with her. Watch over her. Protect her. Heal her body, soul, and spirit. Help her to understand her needs and how to communicate them assertively.

Give me wisdom instead of confusion, insight instead of misapprehension. Let all my actions reflect Your unconditional love and forgiveness. In Jesus' name, amen.

"May the words of my mouth and the meditation of my heart be pleasing to You, O LORD, my rock and my redeemer." — Psalm 19:14

CHAPTER 17

Acknowledge and Grieve Your Losses

"I weep with sorrow; encourage me by Your word." — Psalm 119:28

MY STORY

Like the drop of a guillotine blade, my husband's sin severed him from our lives. His actions shattered my daughter's innocence and childhood. My dreams of a happy family and our marriage… gone. My two-year-old son would grow up without a father. So much lost because my husband chose to fulfill inappropriate fleshly desires.

REFLECTION

We all experience loss at some point in our lives. Maybe a friend moved away or you got laid off from your job or your son went off to college 3000 miles away. The point is someone or something significant to you isn't there anymore. The grief experienced with any loss follows the same cycle as that in the death of a loved one, though the intensity of grief may be different. The stages of grief:

- Shock
- Denial
- Anger
- Bargaining
- Depression
- Testing
- Acceptance[1]

For seven years I tried to fool myself into believing I hadn't lost anything but my marriage. I didn't want to admit other losses — my ability to be stay-at-home mom, a father for my children. Acknowledging my losses meant experiencing more pain, and I'd had enough pain already! (Denial will meet you in many places.)

My subconscious mind was fully aware of the losses and wanted to grieve. I refused. During the ensuing years depression plagued me, panic attacked me, and a victim mentality gripped me. Then one day while reading a book on divorce recovery, I sat down and made a list of everything I lost in that situation. I grieved each item on the list no matter how trivial the loss seemed. This opened the door to further emotional healing.

It is natural to avoid pain. After all, it's unpleasant at best. It's important to see pain for what it is, a symptom of

> **Grace is freeing me to no longer minimize, justify, or deny my losses, but to face them with integrity and grieve over them.**
>
> *~Nancy Groom*

an underlying problem. God created an amazing body for us. We have within our body muscular, nervous, cardiovascular, digestive, and respiratory systems, to name a few. Though you may not consciously realize it, when your child says she hurts, the first thing you do is begin the process of elimination. You ask where it hurts and make an effort to determine which body system is affected. In other words, if her stomach hurts you don't wonder if there is something wrong with her lungs.

Our emotions can and do cause physical reactions within our body, such as nausea or diarrhea experienced during extreme nervousness. Grief, betrayal, anger, and other negative emotions cause us mental suffering, pain.

Because I refused to acknowledge and grieve my losses, my body stored the accompanying emotional pain of the loss. Just as your body expels a splinter embedded in your finger, your body works to expel stored emotional pain. The stored pain is often expelled through physical illness, depression, or inappropriate behaviors.

Refusal to acknowledge and experience your emotional pain prolongs the pain. Like the splinter I mentioned, as long as your emotional pain remains in the body, it hurts. You bear a degree of physical pain to remove a splinter, but once removed, the pain ebbs away and disappears.

We must also come out of denial about our losses. Where formerly we had numbed our anger and pain at life's disappointments, now we must come to terms with our losses and all their accompanying emotions... Grace is freeing me to no longer minimize, justify, or deny my losses, but to face them with integrity and grieve over them. Coming out of denial about past losses has been critical to my healing process.[2] ~Nancy Groom

Don't shove your pain into a dark closet for seven years like I did. Allow yourself to grieve your losses and disappointments. You may experience a degree of pain, but don't be afraid. Acknowledging your wounds will allow you to heal.

ACTION STEPS

- In your journal list what you and your children have lost. Take as much time as you need. You may find yourself crying before you finish so have plenty of tissues on hand.
- Allow yourself to cry and grieve the loss of each item on the list; it's an important part of the healing process.
- Pray for and expect restoration. Be specific in your prayers, e.g. "God restore my daughter's innocence." But don't put God in a box by expecting Him to do it your way. God will bring restoration in His time and in His fashion.
- Put your hope in God (see Romans 8:28), rather than stay mired in your pain or losses. Trust Him to bring new dreams and to restore you and your family to wholeness. He will!
- Read through your promise verses. Reread the chapter "Put Your Hope and Faith in God," if necessary.
- Read Psalm 103:1-5.

PRAYER

God, comfort me as I grieve my losses. Bring healing to my wounded heart and the strength to overcome these losses. Restore what Satan has stolen. In Jesus' name, amen. *(Joel 2:25)*

"Restore to me the joy of Your salvation, And uphold me with Your generous Spirit." — Psalm 51:12 (NKJV)

CHAPTER 18

Regarding Divorce

(If your husband is not the perpetrator, you can skip this chapter.)

*"Unless the LORD builds a house, the work
of the builders is wasted." — Psalm 127:1*

MY STORY

While my husband was in prison the therapy program required him to write a letter of explanation detailing his abuse of my daughter. When he went to trial, he admitted to three occurrences. The reality: he started abusing her the year we began dating, and continued for nine years before being caught. The letter revealed the intricate web of lies he had spun. How could I ever trust him again? I knew it was possible for God to restore our marriage; nevertheless, I chose not to walk that road. I filed for divorce.

REFLECTION

God hates divorce. Knowing that, I didn't come to my decision on a whim. I spent a year and a half fighting with it. During that time I carefully watched my husband's progress. I received that fateful letter two years to the month after he was arrested. In those two years, I saw no remorse and little change. I gave him the opportunity before his court martial to tell me whole truth. He insisted it was only the three occurrences my daughter stated. He chose to protect himself and continue his lies. He knew if the full extent of his crime came to light he would most likely receive the maximum sentence allowed. For the three counts of abuse, he received five years in prison.

As much as I desired for God to mend my family and marriage, I knew it was a two-way street. My husband's letter of explanation, our phone conversations, and regular letters showed me he was still self-centered. Trust had not been re-established. In fact, I distrusted him even more now. His letter of explanation revealed one lie after another. Protecting my children became the highest priority. My divorce was finalized three years after I filed (five years after his arrest). During that time, his lack of change convinced me I made the right decision.

Even knowing all things are possible for God, saving the marriage and restoring the family will take hard work, commitment, and perseverance. I do not personally know anyone whose marriage has survived this crime. This impacts the whole family, and there's more involved than restoration to the wife/husband relationship. Your daughter is involved in this, too. My daughter has stated in the years since that her relationship with me would not exist if I had chosen to stay married.

Because every situation is individual, circumstances may be such that you want to maintain your marriage. Maybe your daughter revealed the abuse after leaving home. Whatever your individual circumstances are, many wounds must heal, and that doesn't happen overnight. Everyone in the family must be considered. It will be a hard journey, but at the same time, don't avoid it just because it will be hard.

Choosing to divorce is not a decision you should make in the heat of your anger or depth of your hurt. Critical decisions must be made and raw emotions negatively impact your ability to make wise choices. Unless your lawyer advises otherwise, I recommend you wait to make a final decision about divorce until you can think the situation through rationally, unaffected by the pain of your husband's abuse against your child. This also allows time to learn the outcome of any trial. As a temporary stop gap, consult your lawyer about a legal separation and establishing child support.

Healing from any divorce takes time, and exactly how much time involves such factors as how good your relationship was before this happened, how committed you are to your spouse, your personality and age, and socio-economic status. Your situation has been compounded by abuse. Allow yourself to fully heal from both your husband's betrayal and the trauma of divorce rather than rush into a new relationship. Allow God to be your husband (see Isaiah 54:5). You are in covenant with Him, and He will watch over you.

Concentrate on helping your daughter get better and letting your wounds heal.

ACTION STEPS

• If you desire to restore your marriage, has your husband truly repented? Is he getting therapy? Is he willing to do what's necessary where your daughter is concerned? What help is he willing to get to restore your marriage? Sexual abuse is a complicated crime, and there are many factors that go into determining whether he is cured.

• Professional intervention is necessary for the perpetrator to be cured. Your husband cannot return home until all risk to your children is gone. Only qualified professionals can determine whether your husband has been cured and is safe.

• When you are past your anger, make a list of the positive and negative aspects of your relationship. Be honest with yourself. Seeing these positives and negatives side-by-side, along with answers to the above questions will help you make your decision.

- I am not advocating divorce, but I do want you to realize you have scriptural grounds for it (see Matthew 5:32).
- If you choose divorce, do not allow friends and family to push you into a new relationship. I see it on TV all the time. A man or woman has been widowed or divorced and the friends are saying, "It's been a year; it's time to move on." Politely tell them "I want a new relationship to be a healthy one and it won't be until I've dealt with the hurt and distrust I still feel."
- To find a lawyer first read Appendix B, "Five Steps to Finding a Good Lawyer" by attorney Laurie A. Gray.

PRAYER

God comfort and guide me. Keep me from making any rash decisions, but rather help me make wise choices. Give me wisdom for my situation. (Ask God to give you answers for any specific decision you face.) In Jesus' name, amen.

"Commit everything you do to the LORD.
Trust Him, and He will help you." — Psalm 37:5

CHAPTER 19

Embrace Personal Accountability

"He leads the humble in doing right,
teaching them His way." — Psalm 25:9

MY STORY

In the judgment against my son, the court required he attend therapy. He was accountable to the court to meet all the requirements they placed on him. Therefore, when he stopped attending therapy he was brought back into court. He ended up in jail and subsequently sentenced to nine months in a community correction program. The best I could do was to encourage him and hold him accountable to his treatment plan.

REFLECTION

"Accountable," defined by *Webster's New Universal Unabridged Dictionary*, means "subject to the obligation to report, explain, or justify something; responsible; answerable."[1] Accountability is not just for those who break the law. It is an important element for anyone seeking to make change in her or his life. Though accountability is often seen in a negative light, it is a positive thing. It's having someone on the journey with us urging us on with words like "come on, you can do it; you fell down, but don't give up, I'm here to help; we're going to do this together."

There is a right and wrong way to handle accountability. No one wants to be raked over the coals all the time. An accountability partner (or group) is there to encourage you when you are struggling, tell you when you are slacking off, remind you of your goal and your commitment to that goal, and hold you to that commitment in an assertive and positive manner, not judgmentally.

Accountability is assertive communication that encourages growth and positive change and places responsibility for action on the appropriate person. Nagging is not an accountability technique. Nagging is negative, unhealthy, ineffective communication. The consequences of the household rules (e.g. no TV if your homework isn't done) and the natural consequences (failing the test because she didn't study) are more effective in teaching responsibilities than 100 hours of nagging ever could be.

Accountability is essential in changing wrong thinking or undesired behavior — both of which exist in the perpetrator and the victim.

In our therapy program, each of us had a treatment plan devised and written by our therapist that established goals for us. Some of the goals were court mandated, some were not. Gaining new thought processes, learning healthy coping techniques, and what constitutes a healthy relationship were a few of those goals. Social workers assigned to our case held me accountable to court-imposed goals and requirements. My counselor held me accountable to personal goals we set for therapy.

I knew the requirements of the treatment plans designed for my children and my husband. Additionally, I knew the legal restrictions the court placed on my son and my husband. This allowed me to hold them accountable when I witnessed unhealthy behavior from them.

Should you decide on counseling, your counselor will develop a treatment plan for you, just as the counselor will develop one for your daughter. It's important you know and understand what is required of you, your daughter, and the perpetrator if he is a member of the family. Although the therapist and the legal system are the primary accountability parties in a situation such as this, you also play a role in accountability. For example, it didn't take much for my daughter and me to get into an argument. We both were learning healthy techniques to handle anger. If she attempted a shouting match and I ignored the new techniques, I would hinder the healing process and allow my daughter to remain trapped in unhealthy behaviors. Additionally, if I shouted back, I would be reinforcing inappropriate behavior rather than modeling healthy anger management. I needed to use the new techniques I was learning and calmly remind her of the appropriate methods to handle her anger (mind you, I didn't always succeed). That's accountability at work.

As a parent, you are also your child's protector. If your child's abuser is not in prison, you need to know the legal boundaries placed on that person and assure he stays within them. If he doesn't, report his behavior to the appropriate authorities immediately.

Therapists are skilled at holding their patients accountable. Accountability moments with my counselor sometimes made me cry, not because she was cruel, but because she made me look at a truth I didn't want to face.

Traits of a Good Accountability Partner…

- Is a peer of the same gender who models traits you desire to emulate
- Is sensitive, kind, humble, and wise
- Is a good listener
- Is trustworthy and able to keep a confidence

- Is a mature Christian (if you follow Christian principles and seek to grow in Christ) who can point you to the grace of God rather than weigh you down with judgment.

Everyone's circumstances are different, but I highly recommend you have a friend who can be an accountability partner for you, not to hold you accountable to therapy goals, but as a mother and a woman. Are you seeking God for answers? Are you taking care of yourself? Are you being too lenient (or too strict) with your daughter? Each of these questions requires accountability of you. One of your prayer partners may be a good choice. As I stressed in the chapter on seeking prayer warriors, this is a difficult situation, and you shouldn't go it alone.

ACTION STEPS

- Learn to be assertive if you are not already. Get a book from the library or ask your counselor to give you some guidance and information.
- Ask your daughter's counselor what behaviors and thinking patterns must change. If needed, ask the counselor's guidance on how to appropriately communicate with your daughter when she acts out or falls back into bad coping techniques or wrong thinking.
- Hold your daughter responsible for what she is learning. Don't allow her to make excuses; excuses are an effort to escape responsibility. Just as you expect her to do her schoolwork, expect her to change inappropriate thinking and behavior.
- Ask your accountability/prayer partners to be open with you when they see you acting in a negative manner. The truth can hurt, but when it is spoken with love and concern you are more likely to hear it and act on it objectively instead of lash

out defensively.

- For further reading on accountability, visit www.disciple shiptools.org/apps/articles/default.asp?articleid=36762

PRAYER

Heavenly Father, You are the ultimate accountability partner. Show me when I respond with selfishness or hurt or anger and teach me to respond with love, joy, peace, patience, kindness, goodness, faithfulness, gentleness, and self-control. When the need arises, help me to stand firm and hold my family members accountable for their actions and behavior. In Jesus' name, amen. *(Galatians 5:22-23)*

"The LORD is known for His justice.
The wicked are trapped by their own deeds." — Psalm 9:16

CHAPTER 20

Regaining Normalcy

"Wait on the LORD; Be of good courage,
And He shall strengthen your heart;
Wait, I say, on the LORD!" — Psalm 27:14 (NKJV)

MY STORY

For four months our house was in turmoil. Military investigators and social workers questioned me with regularity. After the basement fire, I had construction workers traipsing in and out. In December 1994, my daughter came home after three months in the psychiatric hospital. Then on January 26, 1995, my husband was court-martialed, sentenced to five years, and sent to a local military prison. In May 1995, he was sent to a prison in California, ending my weekend visits.

With determination, one day at a time, I worked to restore normalcy to our lives. I took my toddler to the park, weather permitting, prepared home-cooked meals, and read bedtime stories. I read the Bible daily.

Little by little, the light of God's restoration pricked at the blackness of my soul. One hot August night, three years after it all began, I dreamt I was in a massive car accident. I lay in emergency, limbs severed and bleeding, but then I got up and wandered from one casualty to the next. I saw mangled, dismembered bodies, just like mine. When a doctor finally came to me as I wandered the hall, he said, "You're going to be all right. You can go home now." At that point, I woke up and I knew I was going to be all right. The worst of this ordeal was over; the sun was shining once again.

REFLECTION

"When will this end?" might be a question you ask yourself often (I know I did). No one but God has that answer. Normalcy eluded my family for so long because several crises assaulted us at once. I pray you don't find yourself in those circumstances. Be confident in this: It will end. Life resumes and you find a new normal.

By normalcy, I mean what is routine. Routine seems so mundane, but it fulfills a basic need: certainty. Crisis strips away our sense of certainty/security. As women, we want to know the bills will be paid, that there will be food on the table and a roof over our head. Security is very important for your children, too — even for teenagers, not that they wouldn't admit to it. Though young children can't articulate it or fully realize it, they feel secure because you are there for them — you tuck them into bed; fix breakfast, lunch and dinner; and put Band-Aids on their scrapes.

When crisis strikes, our established normal routine disappears, at least for a time. New demands command your time — in my case a multitude of court appearances, hospital visits, and counseling appointments. As a stay-at-home homeschooling mother, my husband's crime turned our world upside down. I would have to get a job and the kids would have to go to public school. So I worked hard to maintain important daily rituals such as breakfast with the kids, reading bedtime stories to my three-year-old, and my morning quiet time with God. Keeping these daily rituals in my life helped me preserve a degree of security — and sanity. Keeping up meaningful rituals from your previous normal will help you face your difficulties. When circumstances calm down, carry forward as many of these rituals as possible.

Try to establish a set day and time for counseling appointments for you and your daughter. Having the appointment on the same day and time each week/month establishes a routine flow to your week. It becomes part of your new normal. Whereas a different day and time with each new appointment makes it seem like a disruption to your routine, adding to your stress level.

Whether you were a working mother or a stay-at-home mom, your husband may no longer be there to help run the household and take care of the kids. As a single parent you will feel there is never enough time to get everything done. The duties you once shared with your husband, you now do alone. Relax. Do not impose superwoman expectations on yourself, and don't allow others to either. Do the best you can, and rest in that.

What tasks did your husband do? Can any of them be delegated to your children? Can a neighbor mow the lawn on the days he mows his own? Do you really need to dust and vacuum every week? Take stock of all the duties you complete each week. Are you doing things your children could be doing for themselves such as picking up their toys and dirty laundry and making their beds? There are many age-appropriate chores children can do. They'll learn responsibility and feel good about themselves because they are contributing to the family. Here are two articles that outline how to handle chores:

"Age Appropriate Chores" by Sheila Seifert at Focus on the Family — www.focusonthefamily.com/parenting/parenting_challenges/motivating_kids_to_clean_up/age_appropriate_chores.aspx

"Divide and Conquer Household Chores" by Annie Stuart at WebMD.com — www.webmd.com/parenting/features/chores-for-children

Pick and choose chores you are willing to neglect to a degree. Is it necessary to make your bed everyday? Can you grocery shop every two weeks instead of every week? Even under ideal circumstances, the job of running a home is never ending. Spending time with your children is more important than a spotless home and a well executed to-do list. Finding a new normal will come with time; don't try to force it.

God saves, provides, and restores. Satan kills, steals, and destroys. God's promises are abundant, and in His Word you will find strength and comfort. "For all of God's promises have been fulfilled in Christ with a resounding 'Yes!' And through Christ, our 'Amen' (which means 'Yes') ascends to God for His glory." (2 Corinthians 1:20) Did you catch that? Amen means "yes." Because we know God's promises are yes, we can confidently say "so be it done for me." He will take the broken pieces of your family's life and make a beautiful new picture.

ACTION STEPS

• Do your best to maintain the normal schedules established before tragedy struck.

• Focus on today.

• Acknowledge and reward your successes.

• Praise the positive behavior in your children, and you will reinforce that behavior. In other words, if the only attention you give your children is when they misbehave, they're going to misbehave.

• Regularly schedule fun family activities. Turmoil and stress demand your thoughts and sap your energy, but family fun and laughter regenerate. Laughter is good medicine (see

Proverbs 17:22).

• Make a list of fun activities you enjoy with your family. That might include baking cookies together, a family game night, riding bikes, going to the park, or reading bedtime stories, etc. Keep this list in a handy place and refer to it whenever you need an idea. The list will relieve you of having to brainstorm ideas when the kids are bored or arguing with each other. If stress is mounting, don't wait for your scheduled fun night. Grab your list and find an activity that is convenient for the moment at hand.

• Create a fun activities list for yourself. Schedule "me" time at least once a month.

• Write God's promises in a personalized format in your journal or on a separate sheet of paper that you post in a prominent place. Use these Scriptures in your prayers and to encourage yourself when it seems you are losing ground. I'll start the list for you.

No weapon formed against me shall prosper. (Isaiah 54:17)

God is able to do exceedingly abundantly above all that I ask or think, according to the power that works in me. (Ephesians 3.20) The power that works within us is the power of Christ.

"Yes, ask Me for anything in My name, and I will do it!" (John 14:14)

I am blessed because I trust in the Lord. (Psalm 40:4)

I am confident, for You are with me. You strengthen me; You will help me; You uphold me with Your righteous right hand. (Isaiah 41:10)

PRAYER

Thank You, God, that You have enabled us to overcome this situation. Renew my strength and guide me day by day.

Bring healing to my family. Bring normalcy to our family once again. Make my children and me more than conquerors through Christ Jesus. Continue Your healing work in our lives. In Jesus' name, amen. *(Romans 8:35-39)*

"Give thanks to the LORD, for He is good!
His faithful love endures forever." — Psalm 107:1

CHAPTER 21

Beware Bitterness

"Answer me when I call to You, O God who declares me innocent. Free me from my troubles. Have mercy on me and hear my prayer." — Psalm 4:1

MY STORY

Life beat and battered me for four years. During those years, I retreated deep into a shell. By now, my youngest son was in first grade. My two older children still battled to find victory. My husband was soon to be my second ex-husband. I felt worthless and unlovable. Like most people though, I donned the "everything's okay" facade.

That year, 1998, I began a job as an administrative assistant for a Christian organization. The first twenty minutes of every workday began with a department devotional time. I liked that. I needed God's Word and encouragement like the desert needs water. My co-workers treated me as an equal — something I had rarely experienced in previous work environments. As I got to know my co-workers, I began to trust them. As my trust grew, I shared bits and pieces of my story. They didn't judge or condemn. They just loved me. And kept loving me right out of my shell. I can't say enough about these amazing Christians I worked with. They played a large part in my emotional healing. (I can hardly wait to see the rewards they'll receive in heaven for loving me with the love of Christ and leading me down the path to healing.)

From 1998 to 2002 I walked through a tremendous amount of healing. I loved my job. I loved the people I worked with. I had been promoted from admin assistant to a junior account executive and then made a lateral transfer to junior copywriter all within the same department.

Yet my life felt empty in many ways. Where was the abundant life Jesus promised? "The thief's purpose is to steal and kill and destroy. My [Jesus] purpose is to give them a rich and satisfying life." (John 10:10) The thief had stolen my joy and with it my strength to fight back. Each day was a matter of survival rather than victory. Get up, go to work, come home, eat, sleep. And start the same routine all over again the next day. Activities I once enjoyed, I enjoyed no more. My desire to attend church waned. My quiet time with God had all but disappeared.

Then I one Sunday morning rather than attend church I faced the question I had been avoiding for over a year: Why didn't I want to spend time with God? The answer came like a bolt of lightning. I could have convinced myself or anyone else that I wasn't mad at God, but the truth was that I was very mad at Him. My anger took residence so deep within me I didn't see it until eight years after the battle began.

REFLECTION

I've touched briefly on bitterness in previous chapters, but now I want to turn my full attention to it.

In all my effort not to allow bitterness to take root toward my husband, it snuck in anyway in bitterness toward God. Bitter because I hadn't seen answers to several ongoing prayers. Because I couldn't give my youngest son the time and attention I desired due to the demands of work. Because life in general stunk. My anger not only blossomed it rivaled the size of my vegetable garden in the backyard.

Once I realized my bitterness, I admitted it to God and asked for His forgiveness. The heaviness gripping my spirit broke and fell away. Spurred by James 5:16 that says "confess your sins to one another . . . that you may be healed," I confessed my bitterness to my co-workers during a devotional time at work. A few days later the Holy Spirit reminded me of my public confession, and I realized my bitterness was gone. My confession opened the door to God's healing power. I felt free. I felt God's love filling me up, my joy returning.

When we hold onto our anger, it grows into bitterness/resentment. I dealt with my anger toward my husband's crime, and I wasn't angry with God for allowing it to happen. My seeds of bitterness were all the subsequent difficulties and disappointments. Prayers that seemed to go unanswered. Prayers that got "no" for an answer. I dealt with each circumstance as it arose, but I kept score against God. He allowed each of these situations into my life. On one level I realized I resented God for allowing so many difficulties, but at the same time I denied my anger. Perhaps you see some of yourself in my story. I hope you recognize bitterness in yourself much sooner than I recognized it in myself. Bitterness isn't always easy to see, and it takes time to grow.

In his article "Overcoming Bitterness" on Patheos.com, Dr. Gregory Popcak says, "Bitterness occurs when we feel someone has taken something from us that we are powerless to get back."[1] My husband's crime shattered our lives and many of my dreams. That part of my life was gone and there was no getting it back. The Department of Social Services and the courts held so much sway in my life I felt powerless about everything. I prayed God would tell me what His purpose was for my life, but He seemed silent on that request. I didn't know where He was taking me, and that added potent fertilizer to my garden of bitterness.

Depression, substance abuse, and illness can be signs we are holding on to anger we need to let go of. I fought depression and panic attacks. As much as I hated taking medication because of the side effects they brought, I finally conceded and began an antidepressant. There's no shame in that, and if that's what your doctor recommends, follow that advise.

When our prayers seem to go unanswered, we must remember there are spiritual powers that attempt to stop God's answers from getting to us. God sent the answer to Daniel's prayer the first day he prayed. When the heavenly messenger arrived, he told Daniel God had sent him the moment Daniel prayed, but he had been battling the forces of darkness for twenty-one days to get through. (See Daniel 10:1-13). God hears your prayers and answers. When you are tempted to give up, ask for strength to continue.

At the heart of bitterness is pain. Someone wounded you; therefore, a vital step to overcoming bitterness is forgiving the person who hurt you. Remember, forgiveness is surrendering your right to exact punishment and allowing God to be the judge.

We can be fully aware we are bitter, or oblivious like I was. Whichever the case may be, the presence of it in our lives affects us and affects how others see us. I don't want people to see an angry, bitter hypocrite. I want them to see Christ, and only Christ, in me.

Prayer, fasting, and meditation are Christian disciplines that shine God's truth into the dark corners of our will. Each of these spiritual activities connects us with God in a unique way and helps us grow in our knowledge of and belief in Him. They also work to smooth away our rough edges to expose the image of Christ within us.

I made so many mistakes along this journey. I shake my head and marvel at my stubbornness and pride — both of which prolonged my pain and heartache. Learn from my mistakes. Avoid the obstacles it took me years to get past. Seek God and rest in the palm of His hand as He orchestrates your healing.

ACTION STEPS

• Examine your heart condition regularly. (See Psalm 139:23) Do you feel anger, resentment, unforgiveness? Are you holding onto wounds, reviewing them over and over like lotto numbers tumbling in the spinner? Go to God and seek your answers from Him first. As you identify the issues, make a plan to resolve them and then follow through with your plan. If needed, discuss with a counselor.

• When we're struggling, it's all too easy to think God never answers our prayers. Keep a journal of your prayer requests — write your prayer and the date you began the prayer. When it is answered, write down the answer and the date. On days you feel your prayers are going nowhere, read back through your prayer journal. Seeing the prayers that have been answered will encourage you and help you to continue with your other prayers.

• Reread the chapter "Just What Is Forgiveness" if needed.

PRAYER

Search me, and know my heart; reveal my worries. Is there anything in me that offends You? Lead me along the path of everlasting life. Help me recognize when I'm harboring anger or bitterness and help me let go of them. Help me forgive. In Jesus' name, amen. *(Psalm 139:23-24)*

"When they call on Me, I will answer; I will be with them in trouble. I will rescue and honor them. I will reward them with a long life and give them My salvation." — Psalm 91:15-16

CHAPTER 22

Learn to Trust Again

*"Trust in the LORD, and do good. Then you
will live safely in the land and prosper." — Psalm 37:3*

MY STORY

The public saw a hard-working, successful military man when they looked at my husband. At home, the kids and I suffered under his demand for perfection. His raging verbal reprimands could last ten minutes or longer. Yet, at the same time I watched him struggle to live according to biblical principles. He professed to be Christian. He served as a deacon in our church. Was that all a facade?

I learned well that appearances can be deceiving. My ex-husband's heart was filled with sin, and rather than confess that sin and get help, he acted on it. For nine years he molested my daughter. How could I ever trust him again? For that matter how could I ever trust any man?

REFLECTION

Trust is foundational to all relationships. Trust is developed through knowledge of and interaction with a person. As we get to know someone and observe that person's behavior, we begin to learn his or her trustworthiness. If we were to hear him or her gossiping about someone, it would call trustworthiness into question. When we are hesitant to trust someone it most often is because (1) we only just met that person, or (2) that person has proven to us through actions that he or she can't be trusted.

Betrayal destroys trust, and it takes action on the part of the betrayer to earn it back. The deeper the wound, the more action — and time — is required to restore our trust. If the person who violated your child was someone outside the family, restoration of that relationship may not be important or desired. But if the perpetrator was a family member, restoration of trust, at least to some degree, is more important. I want to encourage you that restoration is possible.

My main purpose with this chapter on trust is to help you understand how this crime against your child may impact your ability to trust. First let me address restoration of trust between you and a family member perpetrator.

As I stated in the chapter on divorce, I don't know anyone whose marriage has survived this crime. The dynamics of a marriage relationship are much different than the dynamics between parent and child or siblings or other familial relationships. That's not to say it can't happen. Your particular circumstances will dictate whether restoration with the perpetrator is desired.

My husband admitted to three incidents of molestation. That he perpetrated his abuse for nine years came out two years later during the therapy process while he was in prison. This revelation compounded the betrayal and deepened my distrust of him. Once he was released from prison, he made no effort to complete the therapy process we had begun in Colorado, which was required before he could have contact with his son (my youngest child and half-brother to my daughter and oldest son). My ex's actions over time did not earn back my trust.

My oldest son, convicted of this same crime, completed his therapy and worked hard to repair his relationship with the family. He was not allowed contact with any immediate family members except for me for over three years. My son's actions proved to both me and the counselors involved that he could safely be a part of the family again. God restored the relationship between him and his sister. They have an amazing relationship today based on trust. I love my son dearly, and I am proud of all his hard work to conquer his issues and restore our trust in him. I want to encourage you: Restoration of trusting relationships does happen.

Please realize your daughter may have the need to reestablish her trust in you. Like my daughter, she may feel you failed to protect her.

- Be patient with her and remember that your actions will teach her whether she can trust you or not.
- Be firm with the house rules and follow through with the stated consequences when the rules are broken. Do what you say you are going to do. If you change your mind "just because," your daughter learns she can't trust what you say. So if you change the house rules or the consequences, have a solid reason for it and explain your reasoning.
- Follow the guidance of her counselor and yours.

As tempted as we may be to take shortcuts to restoration, I don't recommend it. God has the best path already designed.

The counselors we hired designed a specific program of therapy for each of us. That included specific steps my son and husband were to take to bring healing for them, and answers and healing for their victim, my daughter. My son revolted at a certain point and ended up in a prisoner work-release program for nine months. God used that time to help my son understand his problems and his need for therapy. After he completed the work-release program, he returned to therapy, found healing for himself, and completed the requirements of therapy. When the counseling team determined my son no longer a threat to his sister, we had a joyous celebration in being a united family once again. Because my son completed this process, he and his sister share a deep bond and love for one another that would not have been possible otherwise.

On the other hand, my husband chose a different route. The military initially imprisoned him locally, enabling him to continue therapy. Within five months of his court martial, they transferred him to a prison in California. In California, he underwent a therapy process different from the Colorado program. I know little of what it included because he didn't share much about it. I know it included passing a lie detector test about his offense. When my husband was paroled from prison, he felt he had met all the requirements necessary. Because he hadn't met all the requirements of the program in Colorado, he wasn't allowed contact with his son. Rather than completing Colorado requirements, my husband decided to wait until our son turned eighteen and would be recognized as an adult. This meant my husband would no longer be subject to the therapy requirements or stipulations in the divorce decree concerning contact with our son.

As my son neared eighteen, my husband told me he wanted to reestablish his relationship with his son. I got very upset. The voice in my head hollered "he doesn't deserve to know his son." I reminded myself I had forgiven my husband and deserving didn't enter the picture. I asked my son if he was comfortable with his father contacting him. When he said yes, I didn't stand in the way. But there had been sixteen years of silence between them. The only contact had been some birthday cards that included money for both his birthday and for Christmas.

At first things appeared to go okay, but long distance relationships take extra work. There were no letters or emails and few phone calls between the two of them. Face-to-face time was once a year for a few days. The onus was not on my son to make this relationship work; it was his father's job. The last visit together my husband kept pushing our son in a direction he wasn't ready to go. Nor was he ready to hear or accept that information from his dad. My husband had yet to develop a trusting relationship. Consequently, all my ex-husband accomplished was to push my son away rather than restore the relationship. Now, my son wants nothing to do with his father.

Take a deep breath. I know that was an unpleasant story at best. I hesitated to even include it here. So what's my point? All healthy relationships take time to develop. When trust has been broken, it takes extra work and perseverance to heal the wound and reestablish the relationship. That doesn't happen by taking shortcuts. My oldest son fulfilled the prescribed process for healing the wound of abuse, and the relationship between he and his sister was healed. My ex chose a shortcut and has either ruined the opportunity or prolonged the process. Only time will tell whether that relationship will ever be restored.

Now let me turn to how this crime may impact your ability to trust people outside your family.

If you have a healthy, well-grounded relationship with your father and healthy relationships with male friends and co-workers who treat you as an equal, you can skip the rest of this chapter. You are blessed!

If you don't fall into the above category, please keep reading.

I grew up insecure in my father's love for me. My experience in the Marine Corps taught me men saw women as objects to fulfill a man's sexual desires. My first husband committed adultery. So I brought into my second marriage a strong degree of distrust toward men. When my second husband admitted he had abused my daughter for nine years, he thrust the knife of betrayal deeper

137

than I thought possible. Even after twenty years, a sliver of that knife infects my ability to trust men in particular, but also people in general. I tend to keep everybody at arm's length. This is an area in me God is still working to heal.

You may discover the same thing has happened to you — that there is always a bit of distrust niggling at you, affecting all your relationships. Because you know appearances can be deceiving, it may take longer to establish trust in any new relationship whether a new friend, coworker, or intimate relationship. Try not to let this discourage you. Seek God's guidance and healing and get professional help if needed.

> **Today, this moment, He [God] feels toward His creatures… exactly as He did when He sent His only-begotten Son into the world to die for mankind.**
>
> *~ A. W. Tozer*

If your husband was the perpetrator and you desire to remarry, discuss trust issues with your fiancé and address it in premarital counseling. Any fears and distrust you carry into a new relationship can negatively impact that relationship.

Unfortunately, that same distrust of people can pollute our relationship with God without us realizing it. I can function in the world with a level of distrust, but I don't want my relationship with God tainted by anything. I want to trust Him with all my heart, mind, and strength.

When we distrust God (which is the same as doubting God) we are insulting His integrity. If you promised your child you would take her to the park and she said she didn't trust you to fulfill your promise, how would that make you feel? That's what we do to God when we distrust His Word.

As I've stated previously, God is not secretive about who He is. He makes His character known throughout the Bible. One of the foundational stones of our faith in Him is His immutability. "I am the LORD, and I do not change." (Malachi 3:6) If God changed, how could we trust Him or believe He would keep any of His promises? To be changeable would make Him less than the almighty God He is. "God is not a man, so he does not lie. He is not human, so he does not change his mind. Has he ever spoken and failed to act? Has he ever promised and not carried it through?" (Numbers 23:19) "So let us come boldly to the throne of our gracious God. There we will receive His mercy, and we will find grace to help us when we need it most." (Hebrews 4:16) To fully grasp the fact that God cannot change allows us to kick our doubts/distrust to the curb and trust Him without reserve to heal our wounds and restore us to wholeness.

Today, this moment, He [God] feels toward His creatures, toward babies, toward the sick, the fallen, the sinful, exactly as He did when He sent His only-begotten Son into the world to die for mankind.[1] *~ A. W. Tozer*

There were times in my life when I felt I didn't have the strength to face one more problem or the wisdom to make one more decision. As a single mom I faced times when I wondered how I was going to pay the rent or put food on the table. But I asked God to provide, and He always came through. I stand confident in His provision for whatever comes my way. It doesn't mean I never have doubts, but I fight those doubts with Scripture and remind myself of God's provision in the past. It is a daily walk. You can stand confident, too. Seek God with all your heart and you will find Him.

ACTION STEPS

- Be aware that distrust may be affecting your other relationships. Don't chastise yourself for distrusting someone. Instead, examine your distrust. Are you expecting yourself to trust someone who has not yet proved or reestablished his or her trustworthiness? Is that person pushing you to be more trustful? Be assertive, explain your uneasiness, and ask for patience.
- Establishing trust with the perpetrator will be a gradual process guided by therapy. Follow the guidance of your counselor. If trust is never reestablished that doesn't mean you haven't forgiven the abuser.
- Learning to trust again, in general, comes through God's healing grace and in His time. Give yourself time to heal.

PRAYER

Heavenly Father, thank You for forgiveness and for Your healing work in our lives. Let the words of my mouth be acceptable in Your sight. Where needed, please open the door to trust and restoration. God, I open my heart to You. Shine Your light on my hidden wounds one at time. Bring healing and make me whole. In all this, Your will be done. In Jesus' name, amen.

"Many are the afflictions of the righteous,
But the LORD delivers him out of them all." — Psalm 34:19

CHAPTER 23

The Victim Mentality and Gaining Victory

"O my God, I trust in You; Let me not be ashamed;
Let not my enemies triumph over me." — Psalm 25:2 (NKJV)

MY STORY

It took me several years before I finally admitted to myself what my husband's crime had cost us all. I felt no one else realized the heavy toll either. My own selfishness demanded I receive sympathy. After all, I was the one left to clean up the mess; I was a victim, too. That was wrong thinking, but it was how I felt. I was hanging on to a victim mentality.

REFLECTION

Your daughter is a victim of sexual abuse. An important part of her therapy will be to address the topic of victim mentality. This is a learned thought process where the person bound in the victim mentality believes someone or something outside her/his control is to blame for everything that goes wrong in her/his life. The thinking goes like this: "Poor me, I have no control over this situation; I am powerless to do anything." But that is wrong thinking.

Because your daughter was a victim, she may have learned to cope with all difficulties from this same mentality. I am not degrading her powerlessness at what occurred to her. She is/was a child and an adult manipulated her and controlled her. What I am referring to here is getting stuck in this "I am powerless over all things" thought process.

A victim mentality releases you from your responsibilities — you don't have to take responsibility for your own choices or actions. As long as you remain a victim, you can blame someone else for your failures and mistakes. As long as you remain a victim, a part of you relives the crime, keeping you wounded and depressed.

A crime has been committed against your child. But you and your other children have been wounded too and are suffering from the consequences. Like me, you may feel like a victim. Do you find yourself saying "I am a victim of _____"? You probably don't say that out loud to anyone, but you might be thinking it. We can all fill in the blank with something because bad things happen. A victim mentality tends to make you feel discouraged and defeated. My question to you is this: Do you want to be empowered to make positive changes in your life? Do you want to help your

> "It was not long before I began to see why I was having so much trouble in my life. My mind was a mess! I was thinking all the wrong things."
>
> ~ *Joyce Meyer*

children do the same? To be empowered we must focus our thoughts on the fact that we do have control over ourselves and our actions.

Many of us are often unaware of our thoughts, our self-talk. To change our thought patterns we must first be conscious of what we are saying to ourselves and determine if it is negative or positive. For example, when you try a new recipe for dinner and it tastes awful do you tell yourself, "I should have known better than to try something new"? When you make a mistake at work, do you think "Why did I do that? I'm so stupid." This is negative thinking and keeps you from moving forward toward something better. To be empowered we must let go of "I am a victim" and grab God's truth: I am more than a conqueror. (See Romans 8:37) The New Living Translation states it this way, "No, despite all these things, overwhelming victory is ours through Christ, who loved us."

One thing the Lord told me when He began to teach me about the battlefield of the mind became a major turning point for me. He said, 'Think about what you're thinking about.' As I began to do so, it was not long before I began to see why I was having so much trouble in my life. My mind was a mess! I was thinking all the wrong things.[1] ~ Joyce Meyer

The book *The Little Engine That Could* was my youngest son's favorite book. I read it so many times, I had it memorized. The book contains a lesson applicable here. The little engine has a mountain to climb in order to get his cargo to the city on the other side. He tells himself all the way up the mountain, "I think I can. I think I can. I think I can." What is the little engine doing? He is speaking what today is called an affirmation. According to *Webster's Unabridged Dictionary*, to affirm is "to state or assert positively; maintain as true."[2] The engine accomplished his task because all along the way he affirmed he could. He applied positive self-talk.

This children's story illustrates both the power of what we think, and the power of what we speak. Proverbs 18:21 says "The tongue can bring death or life." In other words, what we speak can bring bad or good into our lives. I want my words to bring life to my spirit and life to those around me. We can create change in our lives by what we think and what we speak.

Affirmations help us reprogram our beliefs. (If necessary, reread the portion on actions speak louder than words in the chapter on false guilt.) Affirmations also help pull us out of negative thought patterns. I base the affirmations I create for myself on specific Bible verses. Sometimes the verse is already stated in an affirming way. For example, Philippians 4:8 says, "For I can do everything through Christ, who gives me strength." Sometimes I have to rework the verse to state it in an "I" manner. In John 15:15, Jesus says, "Now you are my friends." To make an affirmation of that verse is to state, "I am Jesus' friend;" or "I am a friend of Jesus." The key to growing through affirmations is to speak them out loud on a regular basis. For a doctor's perspective and tips on how affirmations work, read Dr. Ronald Alexander's article here, www.patheos. com/blogs/faithonthecouch/2013/11/overcoming-bitterness-5-steps-for-healing-the-hurt-that-wont-go-away/

Like any new habit we endeavor to establish, such as daily exercise, it takes effort. Each time something negative happens, stop and take note of what you are thinking. Is it positive or negative? Replace negative self-talk with applicable truths from the Bible or affirmations you have created for yourself.

Learn to recognize when you are feeling sorry for yourself. Self-pity involves unhealthy thinking such as "poor me" and "this is so unfair" or "I don't deserve this." Sometimes we need to sit down and have a good cry. Crying is a physical release of our emotions. Rather than getting stuck in an attitude of "poor me," allow your emotions to have healthy expression, but then examine why you're upset. Are you feeling overwhelmed with responsibilities? Are you worried about what might happen? Are you premenstrual?

This crisis is an emotional time. I cried almost every day for a month after my daughter was admitted to the psychiatric hospital. But each day I prayed and did what needed to be done that day to help my family through our difficulties. Pray and ask God's guidance. Seek the advice of your prayer warriors. Determine appropriate steps of action for you and your family and follow through with them. The important thing is to take one day at a time.

The threat of depression is real, so I'll reiterate here, if feelings of depression persist everyday for two weeks or more and impact your ability to function at home, at work, or socially, seek the advice of your medical doctor or a psychiatrist.

To become a victor you must rewire the victim mentality thought processes to know that you do have control of yourself and your actions.

Here is an affirmation prayer I created based on Ephesians 2:10, 3:16, 20. You might want to adopt this as your own. "Father, I am Your masterpiece, created anew in Christ Jesus so I can do the good things You planned for me long ago. From Your glorious unlimited resources, I am empowered with inner strength through your Spirit to accomplish what You have planned for me. I give you glory, O God, for You are able through Your mighty power at work within me, to accomplish infinitely more than I might ask or think."

I learned from my therapist the subconscious mind does

not recognize negatives. To the subconscious mind "I will not eat that" is "I will eat that." If you think I'm a bit crazy to say that try this experiment. Say to yourself, I will not eat any desserts today. Now what do you find yourself thinking about? More than likely, you are thinking about eating desserts. Now say, I will resist all desserts today. Do you feel like eating those desserts or resisting them? Whether that little experiment proved my point or not, trust me on this one, it is important to state your affirmations in the positive.

Another tool to help cast aside the victim mentality is to create memorials. The word memorial occurs thirty-two times in the Bible. The purpose of a memorial is to help us remember something positive in our lives — a war won, a great president, the brave men and women who helped us win the battle. When you gain a victory, e.g. you go a full week without arguing with your kids, celebrate accordingly. Be sure to record your victories (and answered prayers) in your journal. The very act of writing it down creates a memorial. When it seems all there's been is loss, read your journal to remind you there have been wins in your life.

Our instant society has trained us to expect things fast. I caution you to stay clear of that trap. When you get a paper cut you expect it to heal within a day or two. When you break your arm, you know it is going to take several weeks to heal. Someone you knew and trusted sexually abused your daughter. That action has wounded you deeply. In addition, you hurt because your daughter has been wounded. This is a major fracture in your life and will take time, patience, and perseverance to heal.

Your daughter and the rest of your family can heal and have a fulfilling, rewarding life unhindered by the wounds of abuse. As I stated at the beginning of this book, Romans 8:37 tells us we are more than conquerors. Jesus is the author and finisher of our faith (see Hebrews 12:2), and He is faithful to perform His word.

ACTION STEPS

- Just as you have a choice to forgive or not, you can choose to be a victim or a victor. Choose to be a victor.
- God has declared you a conqueror and a victor (see Romans 8:37). Say out loud "I am victorious" and say it whenever doubt, worry, or fear assail you.
- Stand in agreement with God for He has said "you have won your battle with the evil one" (1 John 2:13). The verse says "have won," not "will win." That puts the action in the past. Winning has already been accomplished. It's a done deal!
- Create affirmations specific to your needs. Read them out loud daily and allow that truth to penetrate to the depth of your being.
- Acknowledge your wounds and grieve your losses. They are in the past; don't allow them to affect your future.
- Forgive the person who has hurt your daughter and you while exercising healthy accountability and boundaries.
- Follow the advice of your counselors.
- Memorize your promise verses and quote them whenever necessary (see the chapter "Put Your Faith and Hope in God").
- Use faith, prayer, determination, and perseverance to win the battle. "For I can do everything through Christ, who gives me strength." (Philippians 4:13)
- If negative self-talk is a problem, consider reading Joyce Meyer's book *Battlefield of the Mind*. She covers extensively the topic of taking control of your thoughts.
- Seek professional help if needed.

PRAYER

Thank You, Father, for making me more than a conqueror, for I can do all things through Christ who strengthens me. Holy Spirit show me whenever I am functioning in the victim mentality. No weapon formed against my family will succeed. My daughter is victorious. I am victorious. In Jesus' name, amen. *(Romans 8:37, Philippians 4:13, Isaiah 54:17)*

"I chased my enemies and caught them;
I did not stop until they were conquered." — Psalm 18:37

CHAPTER 24

The Power of Prayer

*"But God did listen! He paid attention
to my prayer." — Psalm 66:19*

MY STORY

I prayed and prayed, then prayed some more.

REFLECTION

Prayer is a dialog with God. It is not complicated and can take place anywhere — in church, in the shower, in the car on the way to work. A prayer can be one sentence and last five seconds, or you can have a conversation for more than an hour. When you have a conversation with a friend, are you the one doing all the talking? Of course not. Since prayer is a dialog with God, that means we also stop and listen for Him to speak to us.

Prayer asks God to take action on our behalf for the sake of Christ — because He died on the cross for us. "You can ask for anything in my name, and I will do it, so that the Son can bring glory to the Father." (John 14:13) This is why we pray in Jesus' name. God answers prayer because of what Christ did, not because of anything we do or did.

You might be thinking God knows what we need without us telling Him, so why pray?

- We grow in our relationship with God.
- Jesus instructed us to pray. (See Matthew 26:41)
- Prayer allows God to get involved in our lives and the lives of others. (See Genesis 20:7, Numbers 11:2, 12:13, 21:7; 1 Samuel 2:1 for a few examples.)

Prayer is one of the ways God established to accomplish His will here on earth. Even Jesus didn't go about randomly performing miracles. Someone first requested His help. God acts when someone somewhere has asked Him to do something.

You don't need special words or a degree in theology to pray. The most effective prayer comes straight from the Bible. As an example, based on Luke 24:45 I can ask the Holy Spirit to give me insight and revelation to understand the Bible as I read it. Praying Scripture is more powerful than your own words because the Bible is God-breathed and Holy Spirit-inspired. As Isaiah 55:11 tells us, what God says is always accomplished.

Mark 11:24 says that when you pray you are to believe you receive what you ask for. It isn't always easy to believe you'll receive what you ask, but Mark 9:24 says you can ask God to help your unbelief. Prayer is not a magic lamp, and God is not a genie. Christ wants to glorify God the Father, so James 4:3 cautions us about the motives behind what we ask for. "And even when you ask, you don't get it because your motives are all wrong — you want only what will give you pleasure."

The Bible tells us not to worry about anything and to offer thanks when we pray. (See Philippians 4:6) Saying thank you is a principle to be applied to all relationships, including your relationship with God.

When I pray, I often pray out loud and as though God has already granted my request. "Father, thank you my daughter is healed of this abuse and serves with gladness and joy" even though at that time she wasn't. Hearing the words persuades my mind and convinces my subconscious that my request has been met. Expectant prayer is astonishing. It fills you with confidence and enables you to believe you will receive your request.

Through the years, I encouraged my children to ask God's help even in the little things. Help me learn to tie my shoes; help me pass my math test, etc. These requests weren't little to my children and nothing is too small for God. I even ask Him to help me open jars when my own strength isn't getting the job done. This may seem silly to you, but God is there for the little things just as much as He is there for the big things in your life.

In Matthew 6:6-13 Jesus teaches us how we should pray.

- Begin with praise (verse 9).
- Pray God's will to be done in your life and other's lives (verse 10).
- Speak out your specific needs (verse 11).
- Ask for forgiveness and forgive others (verse 12).
- Pray for guidance and protection (verse 13a).
- End with praise (verse 13b).

Don't let prayer become an empty ritual. Jesus warned in verses 6-8 to avoid empty prayers. Pray from your heart.

Prayer is our best weapon and works in the spiritual realm, a realm we cannot see with our natural eyes. It is the world of God, angels, and demons.

When our military troops prepare to go into battle, they put on protective gear, grab their weapons, and load up with ammunition. They don't go into a hazardous situation without preparation and protection. In Ephesians 6:12 the apostle Paul tells us our enemies are not flesh and blood, but are evil rulers and authorities of the unseen world. Remember Daniel's prayer and how it took twenty-one days for the angel to reach Daniel because the angel had to fight the demons (see Daniel 10:1-13)?

God has provided our protection, and the apostle Paul outlines that for us in Ephesians 6:14-17 (NKJV).

Vs. 14: gird your waist with truth. In Jesus' day, to gird yourself meant you lifted the ends of your robe and tucked them into your belt so your feet wouldn't get tangled in the folds of your robe during battle. Today's application: put on truth as we would a belt around our waist so the things of this world don't trip us up. We need to know what the Bible says so we can recognize Satan's lies. We want to keep ourselves strong with truth at all times. John 14:6 tells us Jesus is the truth.

Vs. 14: "put on the breastplate of righteousness." A breastplate protects our vital organs. When Proverbs 4:23 tells us to guard our heart, the writer isn't speaking about the physical organ, but about our inner man, the seat of our moral character, our emotions and passions. Christ's sacrifice makes us right with God and delivers us from death. When we accept Jesus as our Savior, we are putting on His righteousness just as we would don a bullet proof vest. Because the battle for our souls never stops, we must keep on the breastplate of righteousness, which is Jesus. (See 1 Corinthians 1:30).

Vs. 15: "shod your feet with the preparation of the gospel of peace." Our feet carry us everywhere we go, and God wants us to carry the gospel of peace with us. In the original language the word gospel meant to declare good news. God wants us to declare the good news of peace. He tells us our peace is Jesus. (See Ephesians 2:14)

Vs. 16: take "the shield of faith" so we can stop all the devil's arrows/weapons from hurting us. The verse doesn't say we can stop some of those arrows, no, it says all. I love that. Who is our faith in? It's in Jesus and the work He accomplished when

He died on the cross. (See Galatians 2:20)

Vs. 17: "take the helmet of salvation." A helmet protects our brain, that vital organ that processes all the stimuli that enters our body via one of our five senses and keeps all our autonomic systems running. It is here where we think and reason and conclude. The helmet of salvation protects our mind and thoughts. Who is our salvation? Is man, or Satan? No. Jesus is our salvation. (See Acts 4:11-12)

Vs. 17: take the "sword of the Spirit which is the word of God." Our weapon for warfare is to use the Word of God, just as Jesus did (see John 4:1-13, also see the chapter in this book titled "Know the Real Enemy" for a closer look at how Jesus used the Word). John 1, verses 1 and 14 both tell us Jesus is the Word.

In short, Jesus doesn't have the answers; Jesus *is* the answer.

ACTION STEPS

Read Mark 11:20-24, then spend five to ten minutes praying for your specific needs. Use the guidelines above. I'll get you started.

PRAYER

Our Father in heaven, holy is Your name. Holy, holy, holy is the Lord God Almighty, who was, and is, and is to come. Your will be done in my life and in the lives of my family. (Now continue on your own with your specific needs.)

"Morning, noon, and night I cry out in my distress,
and the LORD hears my voice." — Psalm 55:17

CHAPTER 25

Get Intimate with God

*"Taste and see that the LORD is good. Oh, the joys
of those who take refuge in Him!" — Psalm 34:8*

MY STORY

God gave me the strength and wisdom I needed for each situation. He brought healing in many ways — counseling, Sunday sermons, encouragement from friends, Bible reading, and even in the middle of a Hosanna Integrity praise and worship concert. God is the Master Artist. He picks up the shattered pieces of our lives and gently fits them back together to create a dazzling new life.

REFLECTION

God is with you every moment of the day. He is there to carry you through this and will carry you for as long as you need. If it is difficult for you to imagine this, here is an analogy. When your daughter was a baby, you carried her everywhere you went, whether in your arms or in a baby carrier. As she grew and was able, you put her on her feet and held her hands as she learned to walk. When she was ready, you let go and let her try walking on her own, but you were right there beside her to catch her if she fell. God does the same for you. You are His child and are facing a situation that requires His strength. Rely on Him.

Get to know God. He works in ways that are mysterious to us, but He does not keep Himself a mystery. As I mentioned in the chapter about faith, God openly tells us about Himself. Turn to that chapter and review the section on the names of God. Look up some of the verses mentioned and read those portions of the Bible to learn more of the surrounding circumstances. As your knowledge of God grows, you will gain confidence in Him. As He brings victory over the situations in your life, your faith and trust in Him will grow. If you don't grow in your knowledge, Satan will continue to attack you in the areas of your ignorance. Knowledge of God's truths is our weapon against Satan. (See Ephesians 6:13-18)

Our primary tool for learning about God is the Bible. If you are a new believer, I recommend you start in the Gospel of John. My favorite chapter of the Bible, John 14, resides here, which begins "Don't let your heart be troubled. Trust in God." I can't begin to tell you how many times I referred to that verse over the years. Others may choose to spend time in a book of the Bible that is already their favorite or by starting a specific reading plan. The following link to Bible Gateway, biblegateway.com/resources/readingplans, contains information about reading plans as well as specific plans you can have delivered to your email inbox. This link to Blue Letter Bible gives you additional options: www.blueletterbible.org/devotionals/.

Each day as you begin reading ask God to help you understand what you read. (See Luke 24:45) Don't rush; think through what you read and allow God to bring insights and wisdom.

Another tool of learning is attending church. A pastor spends countless hours studying the Bible and praying. God has appointed him to lead His people. At church you will learn from the wisdom of your pastor as he teaches and preaches. It is also at church that you will get to know fellow Christians who can come along side you in your journey or who have walked this road, too.

I've learned a tremendous amount about God, spiritual warfare, the disciplines of a Christian life, and so much more through self-directed Bible study books and study groups. Do a search on Amazon or wander through the local bookstore to find a topic of specific interest to you. Ask at church about any Bible study classes they might offer.

Every chapter of this book is peppered with biblical references. Go back to a portion that had special meaning for you and study the verses I mentioned. Make getting to know God a priority in your life and discover the joy of a relationship with Him.

An amazing thing happens when you stay focused on God — you begin to see everything in the light of His sovereignty and power.

ACTION STEPS

- Regularly spend time reading the Bible, praying, praising, and giving thanks.
- Start a Bible reading plan.
- Start a Bible study.
- Two helpful websites are BibleGateway.com and BlueLetterBible.org. Each has a variety of tools for Bible study.
- Purchase a yearly devotional book. These books contain 365 very short readings that bring encouragement and inspiration each day.

PRAYER

Bless the LORD, oh my soul, and forget not all His benefits. You forgive my iniquities, You heal all my diseases, You redeem my life from destruction, You crown me with loving-kindness, You satisfy my mouth with good things, so that my youth is renewed like the eagle's. Bless the LORD, oh my soul. *(Psalm 103:1-5)*

> *"I will guide you along the best pathway for your life.*
> *I will advise you and watch over you." — Psalm 32:8*

CHAPTER 26

Know the Real Enemy

*"Has the LORD redeemed you? Then speak out! Tell others
He has redeemed you from your enemies." — Psalm 107:2*

MY STORY

To recap: The month before her thirteenth birthday my daughter, Jenny, threatened suicide and was admitted to a psychiatric hospital for treatment. My husband (Jenny's step-dad) had been sexually molesting her. Three weeks later, a fire destroyed the basement of our home. Three months after that during one of my daughter's counseling sessions, she admitted having sexual encounters with her fifteen-year-old brother, which led to him being removed from our home. Then, after a four-month investigation, the military court-martialed my husband and sentenced him to five years in prison. All this happened in the course of six months. The immensity of it buried me and for three long years held me prisoner. My natural senses were numbed. I knew only emotional pain — pain so traumatic it stripped all detail from my life.

REFLECTION

In the battle I faced, my husband wasn't my enemy. The lawyers and social workers weren't my enemy. The multitude of bad events wasn't my enemy. The devil was. (See Ephesians 6:12.)

159

Just as we must know God, we also need to know about Satan so we can recognize him and his weapons. Satan is a thief and is attempting to steal from you and your family. John 10:10 says Satan's purpose is to "kill, steal, and destroy." He is our adversary and roams about like a lion seeking his prey. (See 1 Peter 5:8) As my pastor is fond of saying, Satan doesn't show up in a red leotard sporting horns and a pitchfork. He is a master deceiver and uses a kernel of truth in his lies.

What does the Bible have to say about Satan?

He was an angel created by God, the seal of perfection and covered with precious stones. But then iniquity was found in his heart, and he was cast out of heaven. (See Ezekiel 28:11-19)

What are some of his names?

Satan (Job 1:6), Lucifer (Isaiah 14:12), father of lies (John 8:44), devil (Matthew 4:1), ruler of this world (John 14:30), the wicked one (Matthew 13:19).

What are his powers?

He can disguise himself as an angel of light (2 Corinthians 11:14); he can blind the mind of unbelievers (2 Corinthians 4:4); he causes illness (Job 2:7), tempts us (Matthew 4:1), misapplies Scripture (Matthew 4:6-7), and has the power to oppress people (Acts 10:38).

Satan once had the power of death. (See Hebrews 2:14) But Jesus destroyed Satan's power over death. Now Jesus holds the keys to death and hell. (See Revelation 1:18) Our victory over death is accomplished when we believe that Christ died to redeem us from death, and accept Him as Savior. (See John 3:16)

In Revelation 12:10 Satan is called our accuser. He comes to God and makes accusations against us. In the story of Job we see this happen. We further see that Satan can do nothing to Job without God's permission. (See the Book of Job in the Bible.) This is the basis of the question "Why did You allow this to happen, God?" But God does not throw wide the door and allow Satan open access in our lives to do willy nilly whatever evil he desires. He gave Satan strict boundaries.

The year these tragedies occurred I had been a born-again Christian for fourteen years. God knew my strength — though at times I questioned it. When I wanted to give up the fight, when I wanted to turn my back on God, I read 1 Corinthians 10:13, "The temptations in your life are no different from what others experience. And God is faithful. He will not allow the temptation to be more than you can stand. When you are tempted, He will show you a way out so that you can endure." When you are tempted and feeling overwhelmed, don't depend on your own willpower. Ask God to help you.

The difficulties God allows in our lives He allows for our good, to purify our lives of sin, and mold us into the image of Christ. Satan's motive is as I stated above: to kill, steal, and destroy.

How does Satan work?

His most powerful weapon against us is deceit. That's why it is so vital we know what the Bible says about immoral behavior and our status as children of God. If we don't know the truth, we can't recognize a lie. Secondly, Satan appeals to our fleshly desires.

How do we fight back?

Our wisest example is Jesus. Let's examine Matthew 4.

Jesus has been in the desert fasting for forty days and forty nights. Imagine the state of his physical, mental, and emotional well-being. Jesus was fully man. He felt hunger, pain, heartache, just as we do. Enter Satan, stage left, to tempt Jesus.

Satan knows Jesus is the Son of God. He attempts to make Jesus doubt who He is — dearly loved son of God. "If You are the Son of God..." Satan says, then continues his attack at what he believes is Christ's weakest point, his hunger. "Tell these stones to become loaves of bread." Jesus responds, "The Scriptures say..." and quotes a specific verse from the Torah, Deuteronomy 8:3.

Three times Satan tempts Jesus, and three times He rebukes Satan with the truth of God's written word.

Satan is neither omniscient (all knowing) nor omnipresent (present everywhere). That means he doesn't know our thoughts or see our actions every moment of the day. He attempts to deceive us and make us question our position in Christ. He appeals to our desire for love, money, food (the list is endless). He can only be successful if we are not grounded in the truth of God's written word, the Bible, which is referred to as the sword of the Spirit in Ephesians 6:17.

Our best weapon against Satan is the Bible.

ACTION STEPS

• Use Bible verses as you pray and let God fight the battle. (See 1 Samuel 17:47)

• Memorize verses specific to your needs. Quote them when necessary.

• If your church has a prayer ministry, ask them to pray for your family on an ongoing basis. You need not elaborate the details of your situation. Remember, Moses had Aaron and Hur who held up his arms as he prayed over Joshua's battle with the Amalakites. You need others praying for you.

• I encourage you to have one or two ladies who are standing with you in this battle as I discussed in the chapter "Seek Prayer Warriors."

• Jesus gave us authority over the power of our enemy Satan. (See Luke 10:19) Have confident expectation that God will do what He has promised.

PRAYER

Father, help me know and see the real enemy when he attacks. Help me remember I have Christ in me, and greater is He who is in me than he who is in the world. I have been given authority over all the powers of the enemy. Help me to understand my authority and wield my Sword accurately. In Jesus' name, amen. *(1 John 4:4, Luke 10:19)*

> *"The LORD is my light and my salvation; Whom*
> *shall I fear? The LORD is the strength of my life;*
> *Of whom shall I be afraid?" — Psalm 27:1 (NKJV)*

CHAPTER 27

Know Who You Are in Christ

"God decided in advance to adopt us into his own family by bringing us to himself through Jesus Christ. This is what he wanted to do, and it gave him great pleasure." — Ephesians 1:5

MY STORY

Even though I was grounded in Christ and knew many of His promises, I grew closer and more knowledgeable through my trials.

REFLECTION

Our value lies in what God says about us, not people. Whether you are in the midst of crisis or not, it is essential to know and understand what God has to say about you. You are a daughter of God and have at your access God's power and resources.

Truth #1: God is love, and perfect love drives out all fear. (1 John 4:18) To believe God is counting the minutes until He can punish you is to totally misunderstand the character of God. Do we as parents wait with anticipation for moments when we can punish our children? Of course not, and neither does God. His desire is to give us a rich and satisfying life. (See John 10:10)

Truth #2: Apart from Christ, I can do nothing. (See John 15:5) In my own power, I cannot live a godly life. It is God's grace and power that enables me.

Truth #3: In Christ, I have both the ability (power) and right (authority) to rule over the powers of darkness. (See Luke 10:19) Satan has no power or authority over me, but he tries to deceive me into believing he does.

Truth #4: Satan doesn't want me to know God. When I hear the Bible preached, Satan can rob me of that message if I don't understand what I hear. (See Matthew 13:19) I must learn the truths of the Bible in order to recognize and refute deceptive thoughts. (See 2 Corinthians 10:5)

Below is a list of statements and supporting Bible references that state how God sees you and what He has done for you. A more extensive list can be found in Appendix D.

How does God see/think of me?

- I am the apple of His eye. (Zechariah 2:8)
- I am a co-heir with Christ. (Romans 8:17)
- I am His handiwork, designed to do good works. (Ephesians 2:10)
- He knows the very number of hairs on my head. (Luke 12:7)
- His precious thoughts of me cannot be numbered. (Psalm 139:17-18)
- He loves me with an unfailing love. (Psalm 117:2)

When I accept Jesus as Savior, what does that mean to me?

- I am justified — completely forgiven and made righteous. (Romans 5:1)
- I receive the Spirit of God into my life that I might know

the things freely given to me by God. (1 Corinthians 2:12)

• I have direct access to God through the Holy Spirit. (Ephesians 2:18)

• I may approach God with boldness, freedom, and confidence. (Ephesians 3:12)

• I am free forever from condemnation. (Romans 8:1)

• I have been given a spirit of power, love, and self-discipline. (2 Timothy 1:7)

• I am firmly rooted in Christ and am now being built in Him. (Colossians 2:7)

Living the life of God is to live a life of transformation and renewal. As a caterpillar is transformed to a butterfly, you are transformed to the likeness of Christ through His Word.

"Now all glory to God, who is able, through his mighty power at work within us, to accomplish infinitely more than we might ask or think." (Ephesians 3:20)

ACTION STEPS

• Just as you nurture the relationships in your life, you need to nurture your relationship with God. Spend time talking to Him and reading the Bible. When you draw near to God, He draws near to you. (See James 4:8)

• Read the "Who I Am in Christ" list in Appendix D. Let these truths take root in your heart and grow.

PRAYER

Dear Father, it is overwhelming to realize Your thoughts toward me are greater in number than the sands of the earth. There is nowhere I can go that You are not also there with me. Better is a day in Your courts than a thousand elsewhere. Thank You, Lord, for all You have done in my life and in the lives of my family. In Jesus' name, amen. *(Psalm 139:18, 7; Psalm 84:10)*

"They are like trees planted along the riverbank, bearing fruit each season. Their leaves never wither, and they prosper in all they do." — Psalm 1:3

CHAPTER 28

The Ebb and Flow
of Emotions

"Bless the LORD, O my soul; And all that is within me,
bless His holy name!" — Psalm 103:1 (NKJV)

MY STORY

Thus the months and years ran together — like water colors on the artist's canvas. I claimed back my freedom one step at a time though new catastrophes threatened to bury me again.

REFLECTION

When we suffer the death of a loved one, we can find ourselves crying at odd moments. A special event or place, a particular scent can trigger a memory of our loved one and our grief comes crashing in. Traumatic events can do the same. A certain tone of voice, a fear that rears its head, any number of things can rip open wounds we thought were healed, and the next thing we know we're in tears.

It's okay. When those moments happen, allow yourself to cry and then take a moment and think about it. Ask yourself what triggered your tears. Is a friend experiencing the same thing? Is something making you fearful? If so, what? Is your child striking back at you? Are you feeling unappreciated at home or work? Are you getting enough sleep? It could be any number of reasons. Maybe it's simply that you're nearing your menstrual cycle.

Once you pinpoint the issue, you are better equipped to take appropriate action to remedy the situation if possible. The answer may be some premenstrual medicine or a sleeping tablet occasionally to get some good rest. Maybe you can take a moment to remember a particularly good time you and your husband shared (if he was the perpetrator). It may mean finding the source of your fear and encouraging yourself with your promise verses and affirmations.

Knowing why you feel the way you do is half of gaining control over your emotions. The other half is taking the appropriate positive action to resolve the why, including reaching out for professional help if needed.

Another way to counter the bad days is to celebrate your victories. I touched briefly on this in the chapter "The Victim Mentality and Gaining Victory" when I talked about making memorials. There will be victories. Initially, celebrate even the little ones. For me it was getting through the week without crying, and remaining calm instead of yelling at my husband. Invite friends over for coffee and a visit. Take the kids to Wendy's for lunch or fix something special for breakfast on Saturday morning. Do a happy dance. There are any number of ways you can celebrate without busting your budget. Be creative. Keep the celebration commensurate with the victory. My son's completion of his therapy program deserved a big party. I took the kids and a few friends to eat at Golden Corral buffet. We laughed, we took pictures, and we rejoiced to be together again as a family for the first time in three years.

In time, the emotional ups and downs will level out. The

good days will begin to outnumber the bad days. Healing will happen. You and your daughter will be victorious.

ACTION STEPS

- Know and use your weapons of spiritual warfare: the Bible, praise, and prayer. I kept a prayer log with the prayer written and date I made the request. When it was answered, I entered that date along with how it was answered. I reviewed my prayers often to remind me of God's faithfulness and the victories.
- Plan ahead. Prepare meals and freeze them (or keep some instant stuff on hand) for those times when counseling or court or life in general has drained you. I hate to cook. Just having a menu planned for a couple of weeks at a time was helpful and relieved me of the stress of "What should I cook for dinner?" each day.
- Read your Bible promise verses as often as needed.
- Do not take on any additional responsibilities at church, socially, or at work (if at all possible). You don't need the added stress.
- Learn relaxation techniques and use them.
- Allow yourself to cry.
- If your husband was the perpetrator, allow yourself to enjoy the good memories of times you and your husband shared.
- Take care of yourself physically, mentally, and emotionally.
- I designed this book to be a guide. Don't read it and then put it up on the shelf. Keep it handy and reread it as needed.

PRAYER

Father, You have been with me every moment of the day guiding me, comforting me, and healing me. Thank You.

Thank You for the marvelous work You have done in my daughter and the rest of my family. Thank You for Your continued work of healing in each of us. In Jesus' name, amen.

"Why am I discouraged? Why is my heart so sad?
I will put my hope in God!" — *Psalm 42:11*

In times of trouble, may the
LORD answer your cry.
May the name of the God of Jacob
keep you safe from all harm.
May He send you help from His
sanctuary and strengthen you from Jerusalem.

— Psalm 20:1-2

Prayer of Salvation

Heavenly Father, I realize I've been living my life without You, and I don't want to any longer. I want You in my life. I believe that Jesus is Your Son, that He died on the cross to pay the debt for my sins, and that He rose again. Forgive my sins, Jesus, and come into my heart. Be the Lord of my life. Make me a new creation. Heal the wounds of my heart and make me whole. I ask this in the precious and holy name of Jesus, amen.

Praise God, you are now His child and the angels in heaven are rejoicing along with God and Jesus! It's important that you seek out a church where you can find Christian fellowship and biblical teaching that will help you grow in Christ. If a friend gave you this book, ask where she or he attends. A walk through the Yellow Pages will yield a number of choices, as will the Saturday edition of your local newspaper.

Five Steps to Finding a Good Lawyer

By Laurie A. Gray, JD

1. Pool of Possibilities

The first step to hiring an attorney is to ask yourself whether there is anyone other than you that might help you select and pay for an attorney. Do you have any insurance that might provide coverage? Are you a member of an organization that offers legal services? If so, your insurance or organization will have a list of approved attorneys in your area, and you'll be required to use the attorneys of their choice, not yours.

If you must hire your own attorney, begin by generating a list of attorneys who practice in your area who have the expertise needed to handle your case. Start with referrals from people you know, especially attorneys or other professionals. Try to get at least three names. You can add to your pool of possibilities by calling the local bar association and asking for the names of three attorneys who handle cases like yours. The easiest way to find a list of attorneys is to look in the yellow pages or do an online search through Google, but an easy step one will require extra legwork in step two.

As you are generating your list, consider whether your issues require one specific area of expertise or span several different areas of practice. For example, you may be looking for a divorce attorney, but you may also need advice regarding bankruptcy laws, estate laws, the child welfare system, and the criminal justice system. A general practitioner may be able to address all of these issues adequately. Other situations call for expertise that a general practitioner is unlikely to have.

2. Advertisement vs. Experience

Once you have a list, you need to assess the list. Many attorneys have websites full of valuable information regarding their credentials, experience, and areas of practice. This can be an excellent source of information for you. However, it's important to separate advertisement from real experience and expertise. Anyone can post a website or purchase an ad in the yellow pages or on a billboard. You want an attorney who is recognized within the community as a competent, ethical professional.

The first place to check when evaluating the competence of an unknown attorney is Martindale-Hubbell, a company that has provided peer-reviewed ratings for attorneys for over a hundred years. All attorneys must adhere to the highest ethical standards to receive a rating, which can range from CV (at least 3 years in practice), to BV (at least 5 years in practice), to AV (at least 10 years in practice). More information is available at www.martindale.com.

Other websites that require unquestionable ethics and recognition by fellow attorneys include www.bestlawyers.com, www.superlawyers.com, www.actle.com (American College of Trial Lawyers). The problem with these resources is that they are limited to the very top attorneys in the country, which means that there may not be any near you and the ones who are tend to be the most expensive.

Another important resource is your state's disciplinary organization for attorneys. Every state has someone who monitors whether an attorney is licensed to practice law, has violated any ethical rules, or has been disciplined for professional misconduct in the past. Go to www.findlaw.com and click on "Find a Lawyer" then "Researching Attorney Discipline" for a list of most state disciplinary organizations.

3. Initial consultation

Once you have several good prospects, call and ask about scheduling a consultation. Some attorneys offer a free initial consultation, others begin charging the minute you contact them. Most, however, will have someone available to talk to you about the type of legal assistance you need and whether the attorney you're calling for or someone else in the firm might be able to help you. If not, they may be willing to refer you to another attorney in the community they feel would be better suited to represent you.

Always ask what documents the attorney would like for you to bring with you to the initial consultation. The more accurate information you can give the attorney, the more valuable your initial meeting will be. Write down your specific questions and make sure that you ask each one. Check them off as the attorney answers them.

It helps to understand the attorney's checklist in representing you: 1) Ethically can I take this case? (Do I have a conflict of interest? Am I competent in this area? Do I have time to give this case the attention it requires?) 2) How am I going to get paid? (Good lawyers choose their pro bono work in advance and get paid for all other clients), and 3) Is this a case I want to spend my time working on?

4. Fees, Retainers, and Costs

All attorneys are expensive. Good attorneys are cost-effective and put the terms of their representation and fees in writing. Attorneys generally bill on an hourly rate, charge a flat fee for services, or collect a percentage of the total recovery on a contingent fee basis. Many attorneys will request a retainer to cover a certain amount of time to begin working on the case and/or to cover expenses not included in their fees (copying charges, postage, discovery depositions, expert witnesses, etc.). A retainer must be held in a trust account until the monies are earned or expended, but a retainer is NEVER a guarantee of the total amount of attorney fees for a case.

Attorneys in larger firms bill at different rates for partners, associates, and paralegals. A partner oversees all of the work, but assigns specific tasks to others within the firm who are competent to complete the task at the lowest hourly rate. Make sure you ask who will be working on your case and each person's hourly rate.

5. Trust your gut

Find out the preferred contact person and means of communication. A call or e-mail to a receptionist or secretary may be free. Every call or e-mail to a paralegal or attorney will likely be billed. The person you request to talk to and the expected call-back time will depend upon the nature and urgency of your call. On what type of issues can you reasonably expect a call-back within 24 hours? Will there be correspondence updating you regarding the status of your case?

The number one complaint clients have against attorneys is a failure to communicate effectively. Before signing a fee agreement or paying a retainer, ask yourself if you're comfortable with this attorney. Has he or she answered your questions and explained the legal process to your satisfaction? No attorney has all the answers or a crystal ball to predict the future. Still, you need to feel confident that your attorney is competent and responsive. If you're not, keep looking.

BIO: Laurie A. Gray earned her B.A. from Goshen College and her J.D. from Indiana University. Laurie is a former teacher, coach, missionary, and youth leader. An experienced trial attorney and child advocate, Laurie is currently an adjunct professor of criminal sciences at Indiana Tech and a child forensic interviewer at her local Child Advocacy Center. For information on Laurie's writing projects and speaking engagements, please visit www.SocraticParenting.com.

* This article is copyrighted by Laurie A. Gray and has been used with permission from the author.

Questions to Ask a Prospective Counselor

Contributed by Timothy L. Sanford, LLC

How long have you been working with sexual abuse in females (or whatever issue you're seeking a counselor for)? Preferably, you want somebody who's been working with this particular issue for at least five or more years.

Specifically, what is your clinical style and approach to dealing with sexual abuse (or _____)? You want the therapist to be able to give you "the mechanics" if you will, of the specific style and approach they use when working with this topic. The more specific they are, generally the better. The more vague their answer is, be wary.

How do you deal with memories, remembering things from the past and such? You do not want any therapist that will go looking for memories or in any way pressure the client to remember things. In addition, you don't want any therapist who asks leading questions such as "Was it your father that molested you?"

How do you keep me (the parent) in the loop when working with my child/teen and still protect the confidentiality with them? What I try to do in my private practice is to: (1) occasionally bring the parent into the session and that way they know what's going on in that session at least and (2) pass along general information regarding the therapy I am doing with their child/teen. I let the teen know this ahead of time so there are no surprises either way. When it's a younger child, I will almost always have one of the parents in the session with the child.

How do you know the work of therapy is finished/completed? Therapy is finished when the goals of the client have been reached. Which means, clear goals need to be established at the beginning and are sometimes added on to as other issues arise, but there's always a treatment plan of some sort giving a good sense of "mission accomplished."

Who I Am in Christ

Our value lies in what God says about us, not what people say. Luke 12:7 tells us God knows the very number of hairs on our head. Who in their right mind would want to know that unless he treasured us so much it mattered?

What else does the Bible say?
- You are the apple of his eye. (Zechariah 2:8)
- He loves you with an unfailing love. (Psalm 117:2)
- His precious thoughts about us cannot be numbered. (Psalm 139:17)
- The LORD is your security. (Proverbs 3:26)

You are his treasure. Rest securely in that knowledge.

Who I am in Christ
- I have been justified — completely forgiven and made righteous. (Romans 5:10)
- I died with Christ and died to the power of sin's rule over my life. (Romans 6:1-6)
- I am free forever from condemnation. (Romans 8:1)
- I have been placed into Christ by God's doing. (1 Corinthians 1:30)
- I have received the Spirit of God into my life that I might know the things freely given to me by God. (1 Corinthians 2:12)
- I have been given the mind of Christ. (1 Corinthians 2:16)
- I have been bought with a price; I am not my own; I be-

long to God. (1 Corinthians 6:19-20)

• I have been established, anointed and sealed by God in Christ, and I have been given the Holy Spirit as a pledge guaranteeing my inheritance to come. (2 Corinthians 1:21; Ephesians 1:13-14)

• Since I have died, I no longer live for myself, but for Christ. (2 Corinthians 5:14-15)

• I have been made righteous. (2 Corinthians 5:21)

• I have been crucified with Christ and it is no longer I who live, but Christ lives in me. The life I am now living is Christ's life. (Galatians 2:20)

• I have been blessed with every spiritual blessing. (Ephesians 1:3)

• I was chosen in Christ before the foundation of the world to be holy and am without blame before Him. (Ephesians 1:4)

• I was predestined — determined by God — to be adopted as God's daughter/son. (Ephesians 1:5)

• I have been redeemed and forgiven, and I am a recipient of His lavish grace. (Ephesians 2:7)

• I have been made alive together with Christ. (Ephesians 2:5)

• I have been raised up and seated with Christ in heaven. (Ephesians 2:6)

• I have direct access to God through the Spirit. (Ephesians 2:18)

• I may approach God with boldness, freedom, and confidence. (Ephesians 3:12)

• I have been rescued from the domain of Satan's rule and transferred to the kingdom of Christ. (Colossians 1:13)

• I have been redeemed and forgiven of all my sins. The debt against me has been canceled. (Colossians 1:14)

• Christ Himself is in me. (Colossians 1:27)

• I am firmly rooted in Christ and am now being built in

Him. (Colossians 2:7)

- I am a new creation. (2 Corinthians 5:17)
- I have been made complete in Christ. (Colossians 2:10)
- I have been buried, raised, and made alive with Christ. (Colossians 2:12-13)
- I died with Christ and I have been raised up with Christ. My life is now hidden with Christ in God. Christ is now my life. (Colossian 3:1-4)
- I have been given a spirit of power, love, and self-discipline. (2 Timothy 1:7)
- I have been saved and set apart according to God's doing. (2 Timothy 1:9; Titus 3:5)
- Because I am sanctified and am one with the Sanctifier, He is not ashamed to call me sister/brother. (Hebrews 2:11)
- I have the right to come boldly before the throne of God to find mercy and grace in time of need. (Hebrews 4:16)
- I have been given exceedingly great and precious promises by God which I am a partaker of God's divine nature. (2 Peter 1:4)
- I have been rescued from the domain of Satan's rule and transferred to the kingdom of Christ. (Colossians 1:13)
- I am complete in Christ. (Colossians 2:10)

Father, You have created me anew in Christ Jesus so I can do the good things You planned for me long ago. I am empowered from Your glorious, unlimited resources with inner strength through Your Holy Spirit to accomplish what You planned for me. I give you glory, O God, for You are able through Your mighty power at work within me to accomplish infinitely more than I might ask or think. *(Ephesians 1:20, 3:16, 20)*

Additional Resources*

Books

Jesus Calling by Sarah Young
The Knowledge of the Holy by A.W. Tozer
The Battlefield of the Mind by Joyce Meyer
Fearless by Max Lucado
The Promise Book by Joyce Meyer
Lies Women Believe: and the Truth that Sets Them Free by Nancy Leigh DeMoss
Breaking Intimidation by John Bevere
The Red Sea Rules by Robert Morgan
The Courage to Forgive and *Finding Forgiveness in God's Word* by Joyce Villeneuve. (For more info about Joyce's books and her Courage to Forgive conference, visit www.couragetoforgive.com.)
Parenting with Love and Logic by Cline and Fay
Parenting with Love and Logic for Teens by Cline and Fay

Web Resources by Topic

(Please note URLs may have changed since the printing of this book. Every effort was made prior to publication to ensure these URLs were still active.)

Abuse Advice

Childhelp, prevention and treatment of child abuse — www.childhelp.org/

Joyful Heart Foundation — www.joyfulheartfoundation.org/
Mental Health America — www.nmha.org
National Child Traumatic Stress Network — www.nctsn.org/
Rape, Abuse & Incest National Network — www.rainn.org
Darkness to Light — www.d2l.org/site/c.4dICIJOkGcISE/
b.6035035/k.8258/Prevent_Child_Sexual_Abuse.htm#.U5Rj3_
ldX4U

Bible Resources

www.blueletterbible.org
www.biblestudytools.com
www.bible.org
www.biblegateway.com
www.bible.com — YouVersion of the Bible to download to
your phone, computer, or tablet.

Blogs

Shattering the Silence, help for male survivors of sexual abuse
— menshatteringthesilence.blogspot.com/

Counselors

American Association of Christian Counselors — www.aacc.net
Family Life — www.familylife.com/find-help
Good Therapy — www.goodtherapy.org
Psychology Today — therapists.psychologytoday.com/rms/
prof_search.php

Family Advice

Dr. James Dobson's Family Talk — 877-732-6825 — www.drjamesdobson.org

Focus on the Family — 800-A-FAMILY — www.family.org or www.focusonthefamily.com

Todays Christian Woman — www.todayschristianwoman.com/topics/parenting/

Christian Broadcasting Network — www.cbn.com

Legal Help

For the best and most useful websites read through Appendix B: Finding a Good Lawyer by Laurie A. Gray, an experienced trial attorney and former deputy prosecutor.

Articles

"Control Your Anger Before It Controls You" — www.apa.org/topics/controlanger.html

"How to Keep a Journal" — www.wikihow.com/Keep-a-Journal

*Inclusion does not constitute endorsement of site or product.

How to read through the Psalms in a month

DAY	CHAPTER
1	1, 31, 61, 91, 121
2	2, 32, 62, 92, 122
3	3, 33, 63, 93, 123
4	4, 34, 64, 94, 124
5	5, 35, 65, 95, 125
6	6, 36, 66, 96, 126
7	7, 37, 67, 97, 127
8	8, 38, 68, 98, 128
9	9, 39, 69, 99, 129
10	10, 40, 70, 100, 130
11	11, 41, 71, 101, 131
12	12, 42, 72, 102, 132
13	13, 43, 73, 103, 133
14	14, 44, 74, 104, 134
15	15, 45, 75, 105, 135
16	16, 46, 76, 106, 136
17	17, 47, 77, 107, 137
18	18, 48, 78, 108, 138
19	19, 49, 79, 109, 139
20	20, 50, 80, 110, 140
21	21, 51, 81, 111, 141

22	22, 52, 82, 112, 142
23	23, 53, 83, 113, 143
24	24, 54, 84, 114, 144
25	25, 55, 85, 115, 145
26	26, 56, 86, 116, 146
27	27, 57, 87, 117, 147
28	28, 58, 88, 118, 148
29	29, 59, 89, 149
30	30, 60, 90, 120, 150
31	Psalm 119

Other Bible reading plans can be found at www.biblegateway.com and www.blueletter bible.org/dailyreading/

How to Start a Journal

A journal is not a daily diary of what you did for the day. It is a tool with numerous benefits.

1) Journaling helps you clarify your feelings and thoughts.
2) Aids in problem solving.
3) Tracks your progress (date each entry).

Journaling is a conversation with yourself just as if you were talking with a counselor or pastor. Write about your situation and what you are feeling. Then ask yourself why you feel that way. Write down any answers that come to you. There may be times when you moan and groan on the page. That's okay. Just don't let it be the only thing you do every time you sit to journal.

Journal in a way that benefits you. I've made lists of pros and cons as I sought to find a solution to a problem, and I've drawn diagrams and pictures. It's okay if you have messy penmanship and poor grammar. Permit yourself to write/draw whatever comes to mind.

I have a wide variety of entries in my journal. If I have an "ah-ha moment" while reading a book or my Bible, I stop and journal. I name the book I was reading, what topic I was reading about, and on what page I was reading when the thought struck me. Then I write down what realization came to me about a question or life situation as I was reading. If what I was reading was a particular verse from the Bible I list the reference and then write what insight I had about that verse.

I frequently reread many of my entries. That allows me to see my growth and pinpoint the areas I seem to be stuck.

Remember, the goal of journaling is to heal and grow.

Endnotes

CHAPTER 1

1. The National Center for Victims of Crime, "Child Sexual Abuse Statistics," accessed 9-19-2014 http://www.victimsof-crime.org/media/reporting-on-child-sexual-abuse/child-sex-ual-abuse-statistics.

2. The U.S. Department of Justice, NSOPW, "Raising Awareness About Sexual Abuse: Facts, Myths, and Statistics," accessed 9-19-2014, http://www.nsopw.gov/en-US/Education/FactsMythsStatistics

CHAPTER 3

1. *Webster's New Universal Unabridged Dictionary*, (New York, NY: Random House Value Publishing, 1996), 532.

2. Encyclopedia of Mental Disorders, Theory of Denial, accessed 7-31-2014 http://www.minddisorders.com/Del-Fi/Denial.html

3. Joyce Meyer, *If Not for the Grace of God*, (FaithWords, New York, NY, 1995), 7.

CHAPTER 4

1. Jerry Bridges, *Trusting God.* (Colorado Springs, CO: Nav-Press, 1988), 102.

CHAPTER 5

1. *Webster's New Universal Unabridged Dictionary*, (New York, NY: Random House Value Publishing, 1996), 693.

2. Ibid.

3. Cynthia Heald, *A Bible Study on Becoming a Woman of Freedom*, (Colorado Springs, CO: NavPress, 1992), 10.

CHAPTER 6

1. Neil F. Neimark, M.D., "Five Minute Stress Mastery," accessed 8-15-2014 http://www.thebodysoulconnection.com/EducationCenter/fight.html

CHAPTER 7

1. *Webster's New Universal Unabridged Dictionary,* (New York, NY: Random House Value Publishing, 1996), 1502.

CHAPTER 8

1. Will Baum, LCSW, *Psychology Today* online, "Crisis Knocks: Building Your Support System," 12-29-2009, http://www.psychologytoday.com/blog/crisis-knocks/200912/building-your-support-system

CHAPTER 10

1. Britannica Digital Learning, Merriam-Webster Unabridged online, accessed 8-14-2014 unabridged.merriam-webster .com/collegiate/codependency

CHAPTER 12

1. Mayo Clinic Healthy Lifestyle, "Stress Management, Relaxation Techniques: Try these steps to reduce stress," by Mayo Clinic Staff, accessed 8-22-2014, http://www.mayoclinic.org/ healthy-living/stress-management/in-depth/relaxation-technique/art-20045368?pg=1

CHAPTER 13

1. Matthew Henry, *Concise Commentary on the Whole Bible*, (Chicago, IL: Moody Press, 1983), 386.

CHAPTER 14

1. *Webster's New Universal Unabridged Dictionary*, (New York, NY: Random House Value Publishing, 1996), 1647.

CHAPTER 17

1. Changing Minds, "The Kubler-Ross Grief Cycle," accessed 8-25-2014, http://changingminds.org/disciplines/change_ management/kubler_ross/kubler_ross.htm

2. Nancy Groom, *From Bondage to Bonding: Escaping Code-pendency, Embracing Biblical Love* (Colorado Springs, CO: NavPress, 1991), 166.

CHAPTER 19

1. *Webster's New Universal Unabridged Dictionary,* (New York, NY: Random House Value Publishing, 1996), 13.

CHAPTER 21

1. Gregory Popcak, Patheos, Faith on the Couch, "Overcoming Bitterness: 5 Steps for Healing the Hurt that Won't Go Away" 11-20-2013, http://www.patheos.com/blogs/faithon thecouch/2013/11/overcoming-bitterness-5-steps-for-healing-the-hurt-that-wont-go-away/

CHAPTER 22

1. A. W. Tozer, *The Knowledge of the Holy*, (New York, NY: HarperSanFrancisco, 1961) 53.

CHAPTER 23

1. Joyce Meyer, *Battlefield of the Mind*, (New York, NY: Faith Words, 1995), 66.

2. *Webster's New Universal Unabridged Dictionary,* (New York, NY: Random House Value Publishing, 1996), 33.

About the Author

In essence this book is intended as a way for me to walk this journey with you. If you have a question I have not covered in this book, I encourage you to reach out to me at Deb@DebraLButterfield.com.

If you would like me to speak to your organization or church, please contact me at the above email with "Speaking Request" in the subject line.

MORE ABOUT DEBRA

Debra L. Butterfield is a freelance writer and editor. She encourages and coaches writers in their journey to publication through her blog for writers: www.DebraLButterfield.com. In addition to her freelance work, she is the nonfiction editor for CrossRiver Media Group. Some of the publications to which she has contributed stories include *Miracles and Moments of Grace: Inspiring Stories of Survival* (Leafwood Publishers, 2014), *2014 Penned from the Heart* (Son-Rise Publications, 2013), and *The Benefit Package* (CrossRiver Media, 2012). Her articles have appeared in *The Vision, Live, CBN.com*, *On Course* online, and *Susie*.

Debra hales from Nebraska. Though she only lived there for eleven years of her childhood, she calls it home. When she was eleven, her family moved to Iowa and a few years later, to Kansas. After graduating from high school, she joined the Marine Corps and served three years at Camp Lejeune, North Carolina.

Debra has grown three children and often boasts "They were each born in a different decade." She has two rambunctious grandchildren. Her hobbies include reading — she usually has four or five books going at once — and she likes the smell of skunks. She resides in northwest Missouri.

www.facebook.com/DebraLButterfieldAuthor
Twitter: @DebrasBlog
Amazon Author Central: Debra L Butterfield
Goodreads: Debra L. Butterfield

* For more information and a full portfolio of Debra's publication credits visit her About Me page on her website.

MORE GREAT BOOKS FROM CROSSRIVERMEDIA.COM

BETHANY'S CALENDAR
Elaine Marie Cooper

One minute Bethany Cooper seemed fine — the next she was strapped to a gurney in the E.R. diagnosed with a terminal brain tumor. During the next few months, her mother Elaine Marie Cooper used her nursing skills to not only help Bethany battle an unseen enemy, she also learned to recognize the hand of God on her daughter's life. *Bethany's Calendar* is a story of fear and faith, commitment and compassion, told with gut-wrenching honesty while sharing unwavering faith in God.

CONFESSIONS OF A LIP READING MOM
Shanna Groves

As she held her newborn son, Shanna Groves should have reveled in the joys of motherhood. Instead, she was plagued by questions and fear. Something was terribly wrong. The sounds she once took for granted were gone, replaced by silence. Then the buzzing started. In *Confessions of a Lip Reading Mom*, Shanna shares her struggle to find God's grace during her roller coaster ride of unexplained deafness.

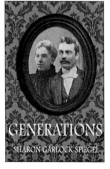

GENERATIONS
Sharon Garlock Spiegel

When Edward Garlock was sober, he was a kind, generous, hard-working farmer, providing for his wife and growing family. But when he drank, he transformed into a unpredictable bully, capable of absolute cruelty. When he stepped into a revival tent in the early 1900s the Holy Spirit got ahold of him, changing not only his life, but the future of thousands of others through Edward.